ACCLAIM

"Chad is a rising star in the arena of sports ministry. I know his heart is for people of all ages and backgrounds to grow in their faith and use their life to impact others. This book will encourage you on your journey."
—**Jason Romano, Author of** *The Uniform of Leadership* **and Host of Sports Spectrum**

"An impactful, quick story that will really cause you to reflect on your purpose and mission here on earth."
—**Damon West, Author of** *The Change Agent* **& Bestselling coauthor of** *The Coffee Bean*

"Championship programs are made up of people of discipline and shared values. This book will help your players grow in these areas and guide them in developing into future leaders for their teams, communities, and families."
—**Brian Boland, Former Head Men's Tennis Coach at Baylor University & University of Virginia; Winner of 4 NCAA D1 National Championships**

"*The Freshman*, by Chad Simpson, is the book I wish I had prior to my freshman year in college...Prior to my freshman year in the business world...Prior to my freshman year leaving corporate America. Don't hesitate to read this book and *implement* the useful ideas Chad shares. Your family, friends, and co-workers will thank you for it!"
—**Ryan Hawk, Author of WELCOME TO MANAGEMENT, Host of The Learning Leader Show**

"Chad is one of the best young coaches and mentors in the country. His heart for training and developing young people is undeniable, and his heart beats to serve. He is influencing young people in

a powerful way. He's influenced me in a powerful way."
—Andrew Nelson, Assistant Golf Coach, LSU

"When it comes to the top people equipping athletes at the intersection of faith and sport, Chad Simpson needs to be on any list. This book is outstanding. As a reader, expect to be encouraged and equipped with practical tools to face your next season of life."
—Brian Smith, Athletes in Action Staff and Author of *The Assist: A Gospel-Centered Guide to Glorifying God Through Sports*

"In Chad's first job, he and I met often at 6:00 am to talk about the leadership methods of Jesus, the greatest leader ever. Chad was a mentor's dream, and he has proven that he not only listened but had the ability to take advice and act on it. That's the definition of 'coachable.' Every coach serious about being successful at what matters most should read *The Freshman*."
—Tim Johnson, VP - Field Ministry, Midwest Region, Fellowship of Christian Athletes (FCA) & 30+ years as the "voice" of college wrestling broadcasting for ESPN and the Big Ten Network

"I didn't see the ending coming but really thought it was powerful! I've watched Chad grow since he was 14, discipled him, officiated his wedding, and now it is a joy to see him influencing the next generation. My daughters will be reading this, and I believe this book will spur conversations about Jesus!"
—Kurt Sovine, Lead Pastor of Connexion Church

"*The Freshman* is an entertaining read that's full of wisdom and powerful insight for young people trying to find their way. I have no doubt that it will make an impact on those that read it, and I can't wait to share its valuable life lessons with my own two boys one day soon."
—Lee De León, Deputy Athletics Director at Louisiana & President of ADs for Christ

"In *The Freshman,* Chad Simpson offers great Biblically-based suggestions for how to be successful in your new beginning. It's well worth your time to read as you begin a new venture."
—Brant Tolsma, Former Director of Track and Field/CC, coached 6 NCAA D1 Individual National Champions and won 116 Conference Championships, Liberty University

"Coach Chad Simpson's book is an engaging story with a life-changing purpose. The wisdom he imparts is rooted in biblical faith and the way he expresses it reveals his heart as a coach. While the book will be especially helpful to college students, it is obvious that Coach Simpson wants to give all of us a game plan to win in life."
—David E. Prince, Ph.D., Author of *In the Arena: The Promise of Sports for Christian Discipleship*, Pastor of Ashland Avenue Baptist Church, and Professor of Christian Preaching, The Southern Baptist Theological Seminary

"Coach Chad has been an incredible mentor to my son. Even since graduation, Chad continues to be available and an important role model. We are so thankful for the support, encouragement, friendship, and the Godly role model Coach has been."
—Luca Blackburn, mother of Sam Blackburn, Simpson's former student-athlete and current Volunteer Assistant Tennis Coach at Clemson

"Chad does an incredible job laying out practical and lifelong lessons in *The Freshman*. This book will no doubt encourage and spur young and old people alike. As a former college athlete, and current college coach I can totally relate to several of the lessons given in this book. I plan on sharing this book with my players, and I am excited to see how it will impact their lives."
—Megan Leuzinger, Head Women's Basketball Coach, Evangel University and the 14th overall pick in the 2009 WNBA Draft

"I couldn't put it down! In this book Coach Simpson shares lessons that every college student would benefit from. Learning to be successful both on and off the court in a way that honors and glorifies the King is the message that is missing in our culture today, but this book draws in the reader and shares the truth of who we are created to be in light of the gospel. A true must-read."

—Tim Sceggel, Ed.D., Director of Athletics, Covenant College

"*The Freshman* is a book I will be sharing with my freshmen student-athletes for years to come. Chad engages young readers in an honest and straightforward way, and the book opens doors for genuine conversations about faith, sport, and character development."

—Dean Jaderston, high school and college basketball coach for over 30 years and Executive Director of Northern Pines, a premiere Christian family conference

"The 15 lessons that Coach Chad Simpson introduces in this book are the lessons that every young person needs to learn and practice. As a former student-athlete in college who has coached many young people, they are the lessons I learned and they are the lessons I teach. The best compliment I can give Coach Simpson is that I wished my daughter had played for him. I highly recommend the book and Coach Simpson."

—Andre' Kennebrew, Trustee Board Chairman, Point University & Sr. Principal Program Lead, Leadership Development Program, Chick-fil-A

The Freshman:

15 Lessons to Ace the Next Semester of Your Life

Chad Simpson

Copyright © 2020 Chad Simpson
All rights reserved.
ISBN: 9798668589364

For Josiah, Abigail, and Stephen, I hope you see these lessons in me and cling to The Way as you grow up.

And to every Freshman that I have learned from and coached.

Contents

Prologue   *1*

1	The Drop-off	5
2	The Letter	7
3	The Deal	11
4	Practice Squad	13
5	Long-Distance	17
6	The Party	19
7	Skipping	21
8	The Meeting	23
9	Dad	29
10	The First Meeting	35
11	The Call	39
12	Waiting	41
13	Answers	43
14	Found It	47
15	Why	51
16	The Senior	53
17	The Funeral	57
18	Big Rocks	61
19	Midterms	67
20	Completing the Comeback	69
21	The Middle	75
22	Mom	77
23	The Mentor	81
24	The Weekend	85
25	Thanksgiving Break	89
26	Final Grades	93
27	Christmas Break	97
28	Weights	99

29	What Else?	105
30	Discipline	111
31	Motives	115
32	Scholarship	119
33	Tristan	121
34	Two Options	123
35	The Final Lesson	125

Epilogue	*129*
Your Next Step	*131*
Notes	*141*
Acknowledgements	*145*
About the Author	*147*

Prologue

No one is 100% ready to go off to college. Leaving behind every safety net and saying good-bye to 18 years of security to step into the unknown. Into a new place with countless underprepared young adults. It's no wonder why so many fail.

Each year, nearly 20 million students enroll in a university as a first-time freshman, but just under 2 million graduate yearly with a bachelor's degree.[1] Sadly, I have seen too many freshmen struggle in their first semester at college. Sometimes it is major: arrests, addiction, fighting, abuse, unplanned pregnancy, or getting kicked out of school. However, at times it is subtle like failing a class, losing scholarships, breaking a friendship, or getting kicked off the team.

I felt responsible as a coach and leader, so I decided to write an engaging story that any reader could connect with while teaching timeless truths. This is a response to the fifteen most common mistakes that I have seen freshmen make. The goal was to help students not just survive college but to thrive by finding who they are created to be and what they are meant to do.

But after I began sharing the fifteen lessons, I saw that they do not just serve college freshmen but are applicable in every season of life. We are making the same mistakes at eighteen as we are in our 30s and even our 60s. These fifteen lessons are everything I wish I had known and lived out when I was eighteen and everything I strive to live by today.

You may be preparing for a new adventure, in the middle of one, or recovering from a failed one. This book is not meant to just entertain, but my hope and prayer is for you to examine yourself. Look inside your heart, write down what speaks to you, and then put it into action.

Are you ready?

This story is written within the context of a freshman in college, but the reality is this—*we all* experience Freshman Years throughout our life. By "Freshman Year," I mean starting a new adventure—something you have never done before that challenges you, stretches you, and makes you very uncomfortable. And if you are honest, you don't know if you will make it through.

But if you do . . . if you finish and complete the task, you expand your comfort zone. Your confidence grows. And moving forward, you will be ready for the next challenge and better prepared to go to places you never even imagined. Essentially, you grow. That is what could happen after going through a Freshman Year. You face the test and your potential to impact and influence is now greater.

Freshman Years come in all shapes and sizes. You could have just started a new marriage or job, or maybe you recently moved to a different city or possibly brought a child into your family. Or maybe you are in a position to help others in one of their Freshman Years. I hope this book breathes new life and hope into you—right where you are.

Personally, I have experienced four Freshman Years at the time of writing this book, and I was not ready for any of them. My first was my experience going off to college. Soon after, I was so excited to be engaged and married to my best friend and greatest teammate. But I was not ready to be selfless, truly listen, or even provide for her. Third, I landed my first "real job" as a small school Athletic Director and PE Teacher at 23. I had to learn how to operate out of a to-do-list, professionally reply to emails, enlist volunteers, and hire staff. Lastly, my fourth Freshman Year came when I took my first head collegiate coaching job in a new state, with a new baby, and a house with a mortgage. I wasn't ready or prepared for any of that.

I had to find my Way through. My whole life, I have been on a quest to learn and grow so I can experience Abundant Life no matter the Freshman Year that comes my way.

Some fail. Some ace.

What is the difference between winning and losing? Quitting or finishing? There is only one Way to truly "ace your life." Turn the page if you want to know it.

1

The Drop-off

Bang! The door slammed behind Chris as he climbed onto the bed of his dorm room for the very first time. Noticing black smeared on the shoulder of his shirt, he wondered, what the heck is that? It was his mom's makeup left moments ago as she left with teary eyes and a motherly hug. Chris was left all alone.

Not knowing what to do next, he pulled out his phone to check the news of his favorite team from back home, and his thoughts drifted to the past. Basketball, family, school, and his girlfriend back home all swirled through his mind.

With his head resting comfortably on a new pillow, the freedom sank in. No one is here to tell me what to do, Chris realized.

Ding. "Make it safely?" his dad texted, but Chris ignored the message. Chris and his father had an unspoken love for each other, but like many men, they struggled to express it. His parents divorced when he was young, but life was quite easy for Chris. He was given every opportunity to succeed and had all the newest devices, but his parents feared that he wasn't ready for life on his own.

Up to this point in life, Chris cruised through on talent alone. In high school, his basketball coaches grew frustrated from his laziness and lack of discipline. Chris never gave more than a B effort—until the game. The bigger the crowd, the bigger the effort out of Chris.

He hopped off the bed and went to sit on his uncomfortable, wooden desk chair that overlooked several other three-story, red-bricked dorms. After searching through stacks of papers from orientation, he found a copy of his class schedule. Boring, Chris thought. His effort in the classroom was the same as everything else. As one of the brightest kids at his high school, his teachers pleaded with him to apply himself, but Chris would not listen. Why would he? He believed he was destined for a big-time basketball scholarship.

He looked out his second-floor window and watched other students carrying their belongings to their dorms. Doubt dashed in his mind. He had heard the statistics of how many fail, quit, or get kicked out, but for the first time, he considered the possibility of failing and asked himself, am I ready for this test?

Stuffing the papers in his book bag, he was surprised. There was a green spiral notebook that he had never seen before. He pulled it out and flipped open the green cover. Inside, he found an envelop with a letter inside.

2

The Letter

Chris curiously opened the letter and saw who wrote it. When did Dad sneak this into my bag? Chris wondered as he began skimming the note:

> *Dear Chris,*
>
> *I am extremely proud of you, and I can't believe you are off to college. It feels like yesterday that you were just learning to walk, to talk, and to ride a bike. I loved watching you develop your athletic skills. But more importantly, I watched you grow into a fine young man. I was not a perfect dad, and I know we had our ups and downs. But Chris, I am so proud to be your father.*
>
> *I want to share with you three lessons I learned my freshman year:*
>
> > *1. Discover Who You Are Created To Be*
> >
> > *2. Choose Right People*
> >
> > *3. Listen and Learn from Everyone*
>
> *Settle in there and let's talk soon. I hope you ace the next semester of your life.*
>
> *-Dad*

Chris appreciated the gesture but stuck the letter back into the green journal and placed it in the back of his desk drawer. Chris wasn't looking for help—at least not the kind of help his dad had written about.

He grabbed his phone to message his girlfriend, Ashley, who was a year behind him in school and already planning to apply to five of the most prestigious colleges in the country. They had their differences. But they also had a lot of fun together, and Chris was hoping to make their relationship work.

He scanned his new dorm room and looked at all of his roommate's belongings. Seeing multiple pairs of basketball shoes, adrenaline spiked as Chris remembered the most important goal of the school year.

The Freshman

3

The Deal

How am I going to get on Coach's good side? Chris wondered before sending a message to Coach Erikson:

The Freshman

A long list of college basketball coaches were attracted to Chris's talent, but not one offered him a scholarship. Instead, he was given a walk-on spot at a small Division II college halfway across the country.

This was the only half-intriguing open door for Chris, so he accepted the spot on the team assuming his parents would help pay, like they always had. But then things changed when his dad lost his job over the summer. Money was tight, and this came with a dose of bad news.

Weeks before school started, his dad made a deal with Chris, "I talked with your mom, and we wish we could help more—but together, we can only pay for one year of college. You will need to find a way to pay for the final three years."

For Chris that meant one option: he had to earn a basketball scholarship by proving himself during his freshman year. If he didn't get it, who knows where he would end up.

I have to show Coach that I deserve that scholarship, Chris thought.

This was the deal. It was up to Chris to make the most of the opportunity.

4

Practice Squad

Last year's basketball team was coming off a heartbreaking loss in the Conference Finals, which only added to the anticipation and electric energy surrounding this season. With four starters returning and the addition of six promising freshmen, Coach Erikson believed they had the talent to be the first team in school history to make it to the national tournament.

The Freshman

"Team-first wins," Coach Erikson shared in an interview that was printed in the local newspaper. "We have to get past the selfish play. Championship teams are comprised of individuals who sacrifice for the team."

Named the Head Coach at 29, Coach Erikson was now in his 4th year at the helm where he was a former standout. He stayed at his alma mater as a graduate assistant, then assistant coach, and finally head coach.

To find who the leaders were and build more toughness and togetherness into the freshmen, the coaching staff planned an intense fall schedule—filled with weightlifting, conditioning, video sessions, and player-led scrimmages. By the end of the first week on campus, Chris noticed he was a step behind the rest. Meanwhile, his freshman roommate, Tristan, was soaring high. On the court, he could go head-to-head with anyone, and the 5th starting spot looked to be Tristan's for the taking.

Tristan's smile and charisma could light up the room. Physically, he was a little bigger than Chris, a step faster on the court, and walked with a cocky swagger. He was the first from his family to attend college and never met his father. He came to college to make a name for himself and prove to the world that he was the man.

Tristan and Chris arrived as freshmen from quite different paths, but both had a blank slate to write their Freshman Story. This semester could be a catalyst—a launching pad into their future. Or it could be where bad habits begin, leading to their destruction. Each had potential. Each needed coaching. But they held the pen to the story that would be told.

Classes were finished for the week and the roommates were walking from their dorm to the cafeteria for dinner when Chris asked, "Tristan, where do you think we will fit in on the team?"

"Me, MVP, of course," he bragged with a grin. "You, honestly? Maybe you'll make the travel squad."

Chris scoffed, "The travel squad? I know I can play with you guys."

"You have time, Chris. You're just a freshman," Tristan jabbed while swiping their ID cards to enter the cafeteria that was jam-packed with students.

That statement did not sit well with Chris. Seeing his freshman roommate impress the coaches in one week was deflating. He loaded his plate with food and mumbled, "I just want to stop thinking about basketball for a little bit."

Tristan turned with a smile, "Yeah? Some girls from the basketball team are having a party at their apartment Saturday night. You should come along."

"I think I have something going on tomorrow," Chris said knowing his girlfriend would not approve. As the two roommates found an empty booth, Chris looked around at the sea of new faces. The noise and energy level in the cafeteria was deafening, and with all the apparent happiness around him, Chris felt alone.

The Freshman

While eating, Chris was distracted by his need for the scholarship. I didn't realize I'd have so much competition, he thought as he looked across the table at his roommate.

5

Long-Distance

After dinner, Chris returned to his dorm room where he, Tristan, and another guy from the hall began playing video games. Minutes later, Chris received a text that read:

He replied that he was with his friends and said he'd call later.

Around midnight, Chris put the controller down and went outside, feeling the thick summer air. He called his girlfriend and immediately heard irritation in her voice and knew that she was upset.

"Well," Ashley began. "When I texted earlier and asked to talk, I really did have something to tell you." She paused while Chris pushed the phone hard into his ear to hear her next words, "I think we should take a break and let you settle into your new life at college."

After the call ended, Chris just sat on a grassy hill overlooking campus, feeling completely blindsided. The dream of a basketball scholarship seemed out of reach, and his future planned out with Ashley was now shredded as well. After a few minutes of trying to gather himself, he went back up to his dorm and got dressed for bed. Broken, he crashed that night wondering, where do I go from here?

6

The Party

Chris tried to forget about his struggles, but he couldn't block them out. He went to the gym to play basketball, but that didn't help.

"Wanna get some wings," Tristan asked as soon as Chris got back to the dorm.

The roommates piled into Tristan's car with two teammates to get what they had heard were the best wings in town. As they were waiting for their checks, Tristan looked at his phone and announced, "It's on! Party time!" Chris knew he should have spoken up before getting in the car, but he lacked the courage.

Sitting in the backseat with his heart racing, he looked out the window, thinking, *I'll just go and see what a college party is like.*

Three blocks from campus, the guys entered the upscale apartment where six girls from the basketball team greeted them. "What's your name?" one of the girls asked with a flirtatious smile. *Meeting college girls,* Chris thought.

"I'm Chris," he replied unable to hide a grin. They

filed into the kitchen where Chris noticed a lot of alcohol on the counter. He wondered, how much can I drink and still have control?

As the night went on, the group had a lot of laughs and played all kinds of drinking games with the TV on in the background. The alcohol ran out, the energy wound down, and Chris could tell that the others were trashed.

"Great meeting you all, and thanks for the good time," Chris said to the girls as they left the house and walked through the grass to Tristan's car parked on the street. Barely able to walk, Tristan took out his keys but couldn't unlock the door.

"You drank the least, Chris. You should drive," Tristan slurred as he leaned his head against the car. The others agreed so Chris took the keys, buckled his seatbelt, and pulled away from the house.

7

Skipping

Sunday morning, Chris and Tristan woke up feeling horrible so instead of working on their homework, they spent the day on the couch, recovering.

Monday morning, Chris didn't want to show up to his 9 am class empty-handed, so he hit snooze for an hour and arrived a few minutes late for his next class where a pop quiz was waiting for him. "Confident I didn't know one answer," he told Tristan as they walked out of the classroom.

Both freshmen went to the gym that afternoon to train. Chris skipped the warm-up and went straight into a few theatrical shots and fancy dribbling. He called it a day after tweaking his hamstring, and the roommates walked from the gym to the cafeteria quite differently. Chris limped, feeling unaccomplished while Tristan walked in his drenched, gray T-shirt, knowing he put in the work.

Never a healthy eater, Chris grabbed a plateful of greasy pizza and two bowls of ice cream at dinner. He passed the academic building on his way back to his dorm and decided to skip his classes the following day. No quiz or assignment due, he thought. Why waste my time?

The next day, Chris bummed and slacked, accomplishing absolutely nothing. Lost, lonely, and wanting to quit and go home, Chris jumped in bed after the day of nothingness. *Ding.* It was a text from Coach.

Fear stormed in like a pop-up thunderstorm. What would Coach want to talk about? Is he upset I skipped classes or could he have found out about what happened after the party?

He struggled to take deep breaths as he envisioned telling his parents about his start. The anxiety overtook him as he tossed and turned for hours. Chris was uncertain of what tomorrow's meeting with Coach would mean for him. His scholarship? His future?

8

The Meeting

It seemed as if his one-hour class would never end. Chris's mind was fixated on his meeting with Coach Erikson. Since receiving that text, Chris wanted to know what Coach Erikson knew. Did a scholarship open? Should I be up front about the mess that I'm in?

The professor finally ended the lecture and dismissed the class. Then Chris walked from the academic building to the school's gym—where Coach Erikson's office was. With his head down and heart rate up, he walked on the hardwood basketball court, under the basket, and down the stairs before knocking on the office door.

"Come on in, Chris," Coach Erikson said as he stood up to welcome Chris with a hug. Coach was about six feet tall, lean with light brown hair, and slim-framed glasses. He was in pretty good shape, and the hug felt strong. Surprised by it, Chris felt accepted.

As Chris took a seat, Coach began, "Thanks for coming. I wanted to connect and hear how the start of your semester has been. Tell me about your classes.

Are there any that you are worried about?"

Chris wondered what to say to his coach. "They are okay. I did mess up my first big project, and these long lectures are tough to sit through."

"I feel ya. We were created to move," Coach Erikson replied. "What about basketball? How does it feel to be on this team?"

"Coach, the level is high here, but all the guys get along great," Chris answered nervously.

"So good to hear." Coach paused as he took a sip of water and then sat up straight in his black leather office chair. "Is there anything that you want to tell me about pertaining to your social life?" Coach Erikson was calm and leaned forward with caring eyes, listening so Chris could do the talking.

Did Coach know about what happened Saturday? Quickly, Chris answered the question, "No sir. Nothing I want to tell you about, but . . . my girlfriend and I did break things off, so that was kinda rough."

"Ah man, sorry to hear that, bud." Coach really meant it. "Breakups are never fun. How did you respond?"

"Tried to forget about it."

There was an awkward silence. Chris tensely adjusted in his seat as Coach Erikson asked, "Do you want to tell me about what happened Saturday night?"

Chris thought, I should just tell him. He must know the way he keeps prying. Trying to downplay all the details of what really happened Saturday night, he began, "Well, I went to this small party, and everyone just had a few drinks. I had the least, so they made me drive, but when I got back to campus, I hit a parked

The Freshman

car," Chris shared, wearing a coat of shame. His eyes were on the ground as he finished, "My RA reported me to the school for underage drinking, and they gave me a fine and some community service. Luckily nothing was reported to the police."

"I respect your honesty. Owning up to your mistakes is a mark of a true man." Coach paused and took a deep breath. "Chris, look at me. *This* is the only freshman year you get. Every day is a gift. Every day is a blessing. Make the most of each day, each decision, and every test. I know you can ace this next semester of your life."

Coach continued, "I want to serve you. Listen, I need your eyes." Chris lifted his head to look at his coach.

"I can help guide you to be a winner—not just on the court but in life. You know, you remind me of myself. I showed up on this campus as a big-shot freshman, made some poor choices like you, and then *my* coach stepped in."

Chris noticed a picture frame hanging behind coach's chair that contained the quote:

> They do not care how much you **know** until they know how much you **care**.
>
> –Theodore Roosevelt

He already knew that Coach Erikson deeply cared about him along with the others on the team. This was established by Coach's sincere personal interest on the first recruiting call, strengthened on the recruiting visit, and solidified when he was in attendance for Chris's signing day and graduation. It seemed Coach always went the second mile.

"Here is what I need from you: first, decide to **Overcome the Adversity**. I know you are beat up," Coach Erikson said as he clenched his fist like a boxer protecting his face. "Life is hitting you. You have internal doubts, broken relationships, and external failures. But like Rocky Balboa said, 'It ain't about how hard you hit, it's about how hard you can get hit and keep moving forward.'[2] If you will take these hits in life and keep moving forward, you will become an *overcomer*. Is that who you want to be?"

"Well . . . yeah," Chris replied unsure.

"Hey, I don't want to waste my time if you're not all in. This can be *the* defining moment in your life. I want you to really think about the direction of your life. What you do next could make or break you."

Chris heard every word, but he wasn't sure how to dig himself out of this mess.

"Here is the deal," Coach said firmly. "I will commit 30 minutes each week to mentor you. But you have to do two things: simply text me before midnight tonight that you are all in, and you have to get a journal to write down *every* lesson you learn this year."

"Got it," Chris said surprised by the seemingly great deal.

"But on this team," Coach continued. "We cannot

have people breaking the law. We cannot stand by laziness in the classroom. This might sound harsh, but you are currently suspended from all team activities. We will reevaluate at midterms. If you have all A's and B's and are making progress by then, I will bring you back on the team."

Chris was devastated. Being the master of mediocrity finally caught up to him. Leaving the office, he felt the toughness in this decision but somehow still valued by his coach.

That night, Chris thought about the path that he was on and knew what he had to do. He was not going to quit. The only way to fail this semester is by quitting. He grabbed his phone and texted coach:

book. He reread the letter with a different lens—with humility.

As he finished reading, Coach responded:

Plugging his phone in to charge, Chris thought, tomorrow I'll call dad to ask about the letter. Then he slid the letter back into his green journal and placed it front and center on his desk.

9

Dad

While it was still dark, something woke Chris up much earlier than when he needed to get up. He couldn't fall back asleep so he went for a jog around campus and read from a Book that was introduced to him as a boy. That day he made it to his classes, grabbed lunch, and practiced at the rec basketball court.

While walking back to his dorm feeling accomplished and observing how green the trees were, Chris remembered his Green Journal and called his dad.

One quick ring and his dad picked up with excitement, "Chris, my boy! So glad that you called! How has the start of your college career been?"

"Hey Dad, it has been kind of tough," Chris said. "How was yours, way back in the day?"

"Not easy," his dad replied. "I wrote that letter to you because I really struggled to find the right path my freshman year. A few weeks in, I felt so lost. So before you left, I snuck the letter into your book bag because I thought the lessons might help you find true joy and inner peace."

"Nice, well, I called because I wanted to talk about them. Can you explain the three lessons?"

"Of course," his dad answered. "Let's dive right in. **Discover Who You Are Created To Be** is the first lesson. Let me ask you a question: how would you describe yourself if a stranger asked, 'Who are you?'"

Chris thought for a couple seconds. Then he answered, "Who am I? A basketball player and college student."

"That's a good start. What would be left if these were taken from you?"

"Hmm, I guess I would be a son and a brother."

"We're getting closer," Chris's dad said. "People define themselves by external things—appearance, jobs, or social media following. But I'll be real with you, all of that can be taken from you. Injuries end sports careers. A loved one could die. Breakups, getting fired, and aging can take away what you are leaning on. If you trust in these false identities, you will be crushed time after time searching for the next thing to cling tightly to. I want you to find something solid—*unshakable*. No matter how much success you have in life or if it all comes crashing down and you lose everything, who you *really* are—your identity—should remain the same."

His dad continued, "When I went off to college, I had absolutely no clue who I was. Too many people want to tell you *who* to be, *what* to do, and *how* to live your life, but you are an adult now. This is *your* life. You would be robbing this world by copying someone else's life. Don't be an echo of someone else.

Trust the voice inside your heart and have the courage to live the life you were created to live."

Chris climbed the stairs of his dormitory while responding to his father, "That is good stuff, Dad. I guess I don't really know who I am or what I am on earth to do." Chris opened his door to find Tristan watching something on his phone with his earbuds in. "What about lesson #2?" Chris asked his dad.

"**Choose Right People**—bad company corrupts good character.[1] You must find a band of brothers to go through life with."

Chris had always wanted a friend who would be like a brother.

His dad continued as Chris glanced at himself in the mirror, "Are you choosing to be close with encouraging people who put positive peer pressure on you? Or are you choosing to go along with the crowd? Son, it's *too* easy to just go along with the crowd."

"I haven't really found any great friends," Chris shared softly, making sure Tristan couldn't hear. "How do you find the right people?"

"It is hard. Life is full of choices, and you get to choose who you spend your time with. Look at the troublemakers on your hall. I bet they all found each other within the first week of school. The fastest way to lose sight of your identity is by walking with the wrong crowd," Chris's dad said boldly. "But once you find a good friend, be a good friend. Listen, encourage, and spur him on. Finding the right people for your inner circle is *key*. This will make *all* the difference."

"Thanks for sharing, Dad. But hey, I'm just about

out of time. What about the third lesson from your letter?"

Listen and Learn from Everyone," his father began. "Listening is *so* important. How would you rate yourself as a listener? Leadership guru John Maxwell says, 'Mature leaders listen, learn, and then they lead.'[2] At the start of your new adventure, ask questions, listen, and learn from everyone. If you find a strong leader, pick their brains about their journey, habits, and beliefs . . ."

Chris interrupted, "What if the person isn't admirable or worth following?"

"Learn from them," his dad responded. "Take note of why you don't respect them. How do they make you feel? What would you do if you were in their shoes? There is something you can learn from everyone. Sometimes, you are learning what *not* to do."

"I've never thought about learning from a bad leader," Chris said and thought of a few bad leaders he had been around.

"You are wired to be a leader. At this stage in your life, learn as much as possible. Write down the lessons you learn this semester and who taught them to you. That's why I put the green notebook in your bag. If you write things down, you are *much* more likely to remember them later. Be teachable, son. Your lessons could come from anyone so **Listen and Learn from Everyone**."

"My coach gave me that same challenge! I have a lot to learn this semester, but Dad, I gotta go. The guys are about to head down for dinner," Chris said as he looked in the mirror one last time to make sure his hair looked alright.

"You bet. Call me anytime," his father ended with sincerity.

After dinner, he sat at his desk where he picked up the letter again and looked at the three lessons. **Choose Right People**, Chris told himself as he decided Tristan might not be the best influence. "**Listen and Learn from Everyone**," Chris read aloud while flipping his pen through his fingers and thinking about who else might teach him this semester.

He opened his Green Journal to the first page and began writing down the major lessons from this semester. The three lessons from his dad's letter and Coach's challenge to **Overcome Adversity** seemed like a good place to start.

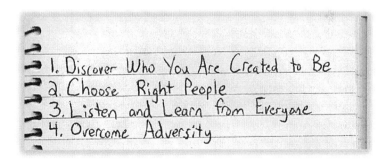

Chris really liked how the day played out and was excited about his future. But challenges were lurking.

The Freshman

The pressure was like a book bag full of bricks. He carried the heavy weight of getting back on the team, passing his classes, choosing a major, and hopefully, earning a scholarship for next season.

10

The First Meeting

The morning of his first mentoring meeting, Chris checked his bank account and was feeling stressed by his financial situation. He wondered, should I be 100% real with Coach? Coach Erikson controlled the scholarship for his sophomore year, and before this, Chris never had to talk to a coach about anything other than sports.

Chris walked quickly toward Coach's office, took a deep breath, and knocked on the door. Immediately, Coach Erikson pushed pause to the practice film on his office TV, stood up with a big smile, and gave Chris a strong hug.

"I was so pumped when I read your text that you are all in!" Coach Erikson said. They talked about what they both did over the weekend before Coach asked, "What's been your biggest challenge this week?"

Chris looked to the ground, thinking about how to answer and said, "Well, my dad challenged me to **Choose Right People**. I have been thinking a lot about the guys on the team and on my hall, and I'm realizing positive friends will be tough to find."

"Man, that is gold right there. Show me your friends and I will show you your future. I really hope you can find that one friend who will stick closer than a brother," Coach Erikson responded as he reached into his desk and pulled out a few papers stapled together. "Take a look at this. I call it *Making a Comeback*. There are five steps, and we will tackle one lesson each week. In between each meeting, you will have homework to do on your own."

Coach handed Chris the papers and continued talking while Chris flipped through them.

"You already have a head start on this comeback by listening to your father's wisdom to surround yourself with positive friends and deciding to **Overcome Adversity**. That is the first step in *Making a Comeback*. I do have an important question to ask you though."

Coach Erikson paused. "*Who* are you?" he asked slowly. "What is *your* identity? You lost your spot on the team and your girlfriend. What's left?"

"Tough one. Honestly, I don't know," Chris answered. "I felt so lost and broken the week of the party. That was the lowest I have ever been."

Coach quickly fired back, "Tell me, how did you respond?"

"You told me to **Overcome the Adversity**. And now I am here trying to figure it all out."

"Chris! You are on the right path! You want to know how to find who you are created to be? Step 2 to *Making A Comeback* is **Consistently Disconnect to Question, Think, and Write**. Did you know that people touch their phones thousands of times a day, and we waste *hours* every day on the Internet?" Coach asked as he waved his cell phone in the air.

Chris considered all the time he spent on his phone. I probably check my phone every five minutes or so, he thought. He snapped back to pay attention to Coach Erikson.

"No one, not my generation or yours, takes time to be quiet and think anymore. We are so busy from dings, texts, tweets, and snaps. This distraction is hindering people from thinking deeply. So your homework is to be alone for 20 to 30 minutes a day to ask yourself life's toughest questions."

Coach Erikson continued, "We need to ask *tough* questions. What is my purpose in life? Who created the world? Why does evil exist? Why do bad things happen to good people? Is there an afterlife? A God? Many gods? Think about the answers. Ask your friends and read from various authors. Socrates said, 'The unexamined life is not worth living.'[2] Write down your inner doubts and findings. I want you to go on a quest to find yourself and the answers to life's questions." Coach Erikson was excited in issuing the challenge.

Chris was locked into his Coach and replied, "Challenge accepted."

"Great! I will see you next Monday at 11:30," Coach Erikson concluded as Chris moved toward the door.

Leaving the first meeting with his Coach, Chris was confident that he would find his purpose. He was so zoned in to finding himself that he forgot about his empty bank account and the stress surrounding his scholarship.

With rain clouds creeping in on his way to lunch, Chris's deep thoughts were interrupted by one of those dings. His fourteen-year-old sister texted:

Immediately, he called her.

11

The Call

His mom picked up, but her voice did not sound joyful.

"Mom, what's up? What's wrong?"

"Chris, it's your grandpa. I don't know how to say this, but . . . he . . . he passed away," she informed him with a shaky voice.

"Are you serious?" Chris asked stunned as he stopped along the walkway. "What happened?"

"He had a heart attack this morning. They rushed him to the hospital, but he didn't make it. I am just getting to grandma's house so I'm going to have to call you later. Pray for grandma. Love ya," she said and hung up before Chris could ask another question or tell his mom he loved her.

Sitting on a school logoed bench in shock, Chris tried to process the news. He felt horrible for his mom to lose a parent, but if he was honest with himself, he really didn't know his grandpa that well. His grandparents lived on the other side of town, but they were never that close to him. *I should have stopped* by his house more or at least called him more, Chris told himself.

The devastating news left Chris without an appetite. He walked around campus and listened to a voicemail his grandpa had left before leaving for college. Hearing his grandpa's voice was not easy, and it made Chris start to think about where his grandfather was after dying. Chris wondered, is that it? We are born. We grow up. Have a family. Make some money and then die. There must be more to life than this.

Chris had to find answers.

12

Waiting

Chris could not stop thinking about the purpose of life. Tuesday through Friday, Chris found 30 minutes each day to completely disconnect. He used that time to question, think, and write.

Friday night, Chris walked through the long hallway to get to his room. He pulled his key from his lanyard to unlock the door and entered his room that still felt like a stranger's house. As Chris got ready for bed, he reflected on his week. I disconnected daily like Coach told me. He also asked a few professors and classmates life's deepest questions. But none of their answers spoke to his heart. He knew there was something more, waiting to be discovered.

Sitting in his bed, he pulled his Green Journal from his book bag and began to reread his lessons.

The Freshman

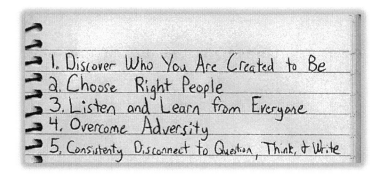

He cried out in his heart, God, are you there? Can you answer any of these questions? I need answers. He tossed his journal on the floor, turned off the lights, and jumped back into bed, pulling his navy-blue comforter up to his chin.

13

Answers

Ding. Ding. Still sleeping, Chris realized it was his phone making the noise. Really Coach, at seven o'clock in the morning? Chris thought before reading the first text:

Coach Erikson

Today 7:06 AM

Chris, you were on my heart this morning. Look up these verses. Maybe they will help you.

Chris fell back asleep, but when he finally got out of bed, he realized he didn't have anything to do. I'll disconnect one more day. This time, I'll stay until I get an answer, Chris told himself.

He found a quiet spot beside a lake—about 15 minutes out from campus that a professor had told him about. There was not another person in sight, and this spot truly was the perfect place to withdraw. On a beat-up wooden park bench, Chris stretched out on his back and stared up at the clouds. He tried to quiet his mind and just be still, but his thoughts wandered.

He stood up to get his phone out from the pocket of his shorts and reread the message from Coach. Desperate, he began to look up the verses that Coach sent:

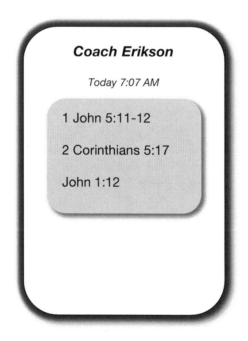

After reading each one, he thought about what each might mean, and why his Coach chose those three. As he focused on them, it was like they spoke to him. He wrote down his decision and whispered, "This is it."

The Freshman

14

Found It

Shoulder to shoulder, Chris tried to make his way through the congested hallway. His final class of the morning had just let out, and Chris couldn't wait to tell Coach Erikson about his decision.

Coach and the team were gearing up for their first official practice, and fall recruiting visits were in full swing. Needless to say, Coach Erikson had a lot on his plate.

Eager to share the news, Chris knocked on the door that was just cracked open and entered the office with more than just a positive attitude.

"Hey, Chris, come on in," Coach Erikson said as he closed his weekly planner and set it to the side. "You seem brighter. Is something different? Maybe a new haircut?"

"Coach, a week ago today my grandpa actually passed away, and it made me rethink what life is all about. So every day I did what you told me to do in Step 2 to *Making a Comeback*: **Consistently Disconnect to Question, Think, and Write**, and finally, the morning you texted me the Bible quotes, it all came together. I know who I am created to be!"

"I am so sorry to hear about your grandpa," Coach said with empathy in his eyes. Then his face turned hopeful as he asked, "Tell me about finding who you are created to be."

They discussed what Chris read that lead him to his revelation about the world and his place in it. This was why Coach Erikson was a coach—to be a guide for young men to find The Way.

"You are ready for the 3rd Step of *Making a Comeback*. **Live for a Y Bigger than u.**" Coach Erikson paused while Chris considered what kind of 'Y' Coach was talking about.

"Young people are always asked the question, 'What are you going to . . . '" Coach waited.

Realizing this was not rhetorical, Chris answered, "Do."

"Yes, what are you going to do? *What* are you going to do for work? *What* are you going to study? Those aren't bad questions, but if we only center on 'what' and 'do,' we will find a task or job. The powerful question is, 'Why?' This stirs up within you a calling, a mission," Coach shared while Chris tried to understand why the *why* was so important. "And people will work for a What, but they will give their lives to a Why.[1] *Why* are you here?" Coach Erikson asked.

"I have no idea, Coach. Why am I here?" Chris said, struggling to spit out the words. "I guess I am studying to get a degree."

"That is fine. Here's your homework; I want you to write a purpose statement. My purpose on earth is: _____. And I'll give you a hint, your 'Y' must be bigger than 'u'—bigger than Chris. Let your 'Why' transcend 'you.' Most people think their purpose centers on self, but there is something greater to live for," Coach Erikson stated.

Chris agreed to do the purpose-finding homework, and leaving the office, he thanked his coach for his time. Before getting too far down the hallway, Chris remembered one last thing he wanted to tell his Coach. He turned and ran back toward the office.

"Sorry Coach, but there's one more thing," Chris said. "After I realized my identity the other day, like who I am, I want everyone to know it." He began to smile with excitement. "So, I want to go by my given name now."

His coach replied, "What did your parents name you? I'll call you whatever you want."

"It's Christian," he said beaming.

"Wow! Love it! See you next week, Christian," Coach said smiling and humbled to play a role in Christian's freshman story.

The Freshman

15

Why

Christian left the building and walked along the beautiful brick pathway that extended across campus. As he passed by student after student along the crowded path, he reflected on the poor start to his freshman year. He failed in his relationships and in his choices. Then he thought about how Coach Erikson entered his life and gave him tough love when he needed it most. Coach also gave him a plan—the five steps to *Making a Comeback*. Three weeks into Christian's comeback and his life seemed to be trending with an upward trajectory.

When Christian made it back into his dorm room, he sat at his messy desk and pulled out the Green Journal. Then he wrote down the next lesson from Coach Erikson:

> 1. Discover Who You Are Created to Be
> 2. Choose Right People
> 3. Listen and Learn from Everyone
> 4. Overcome Adversity
> 5. Consistently Disconnect to Question, Think, & Write
> 6. Live for a Y Bigger than u

Man, Christian thought, six lessons so far. How many will I learn this year?

Friday, he needed to drive back to his hometown to attend his grandpa's funeral. He was not sure how to find his Why, but he supposed he'd have eight hours in the car to figure it out.

16

The Senior

The day before his long drive home, Christian woke up early. He began his morning routine so he could retreat to a quiet place away from people, technology, and distractions. It was his favorite hour of the day. At the start of the year and all through high school, he would sleep until the last possible minute and rush out the door stressed and without breakfast. Today, he walked peacefully to the cafeteria and arrived early to his first class, where he was attentive, interactive, and took good notes.

After lunch, Christian was still intentional with his time, unlike most of the guys on the hall. He was putting in the work at the rec basketball courts, and if his homework was complete, Christian began learning from books and podcasts. **Listen and Learn from Everyone**, he told himself.

With his assignment from Coach on his mind, he researched how to write a purpose statement. He knew it was important but wasn't sure how to figure his out and write it down.

The Freshman

Knock, Knock….Knock, Knock, Knock. His thoughts were disrupted as he looked up from his laptop. Before he could stand up to open the door, a big guy with a bigger smile entered.

"Chris, what's up my man?" Andre said as he gave Christian a "bro hug."

Andre was a senior captain on the football team and lived two rooms away on Christian's hall. At 6 feet 6 inches and curly blonde hair, the guy was a beast of an athlete. Since meeting at an athletics cookout at the start of the year, Christian knew he wanted to be like Andre. He recently realized it was because Andre had such a big heart for others and made everyone feel like they were a best friend.

"Nothing much," Christian responded, surprised that an upperclassman remembered his name and would want to talk with a freshman. "What about you?"

"I have an assignment for one of my upper-level business classes," Andre answered. "Do you have a couple of minutes for a quiz?"

"Sure!" Christian said.

"Okay, we are learning about the importance of a mission statement. Leaders say a mission statement should be the driving force of an organization." Andre spoke with clarity while Christian sat back down in his desk chair and listened.

Andre continued, "Many organizations don't have a good mission statement or fail to communicate it with their employees. So I am going to read ten mission statements and see if you can name the business it belongs to."

Christian was ready. "Bring it."

"OK, Chris, here is the first one. 'We save people money so they can live better.'"[1]

"Walmart, 1 for 1. Easiest quiz I have had so far in college!" Christian joked. He wanted to tell his friends about his name change, but he wasn't sure how.

Andre shared the next mission, "'To be our customers' favorite place and way to eat and drink.'"[2]

"Not sure. Whose is that?" Christian asked.

"That is McDonalds. 1 for 2. Try this one, 'Our mission: to inspire and nurture the human spirit—one person, one cup and one neighborhood at a time.'"[3]

"Maybe Starbucks?" Christian said with doubt.

"Nice! 2 for 3. Next: 'To organize the world's information and make it universally accessible and useful,'"[4] Andre waited.

"That has to be Google," Christian said.

"Correct. How about, 'To create a better everyday life for the many people.'"[5]

"No clue."

"That is from IKEA," Andre informed and continued the quiz with Christian guessing correctly on half. "You got 5 for 10! Thanks for your help."

Christian politely responded, "Glad to help. Those all seem so simple, easy to remember, and inspiring."

"For sure," Andre said. "Listen to this quote my professor shared by Simon Sinek: 'Very few people or companies can clearly articulate WHY they do WHAT they do. WHY does your company exist? WHY do you get out of bed every morning? And WHY should anyone care?'"[7]

"The timing of your quiz is perfect. I have been

working to craft my personal purpose statement. Like those businesses, I want to create a short, powerful phrase that drives me as I am discovering who I am created to be."

"Nice! I had to discover who I wanted to be freshman year as well. A few weeks into the semester, I realized it and turned from the way I used to live," Andre said with a smile. "Let's grab dinner soon to keep this conversation going."

Christian could tell that he really meant it.

17

The Funeral

After his Friday classes, Christian walked to the parking lot to pack his car and drive home for his grandpa's funeral. He threw his dirty clothes from the past two weeks in the trunk, set his only suit in the back seat, and placed some snacks in the passenger seat. After tapping his phone to begin his "Road trip" playlist, he turned his key to start the car. He owned a small car that had over 190,000 miles on it, and it had been giving him some trouble since summer. Ironically, his grandfather had bought it as a gift on his sixteenth birthday.

"You cannot be serious!" Christian fumed. After several failed attempts to start the car, he called to have it towed to a local mechanic. By closing time, they were still not able to diagnose the problem.

"I can't believe I am going to miss the funeral," Christian grumbled as his attitude went sour. His family looked for flights that evening, but they were unable to find any last minute.

Waking up in his dorm room the next day, he was still in a bad mood. He bummed around until a quote spoke to him while scrolling through Instagram.

> **James 1:2-4**
>
> Consider it pure joy whenever you face trials of any kind. Because you know that the testing of your faith develops perseverance. Let perseverance finish its work so that you may be mature and complete not lacking anything.[1]

How am I supposed to have pure joy in the face of adversity? How many hardships will I face this semester? he thought as he washed his face. After drying with a towel, he wrote on a sticky note—**Overcome Adversity**, Again Today. This lesson wasn't a "one and done" type of lesson. He needed the reminder to overcome every day so he took the note and stuck it on the mirror in his room.

Pulling out his laptop, he searched for and found his grandpa's obituary online. Unsettled by what it said, he read some, thought, and wrote in his Green Journal:

> Is that it?
> We grow up, get married, have a family, work for 40 years, play golf and watch the news, then say goodbye? We leave some money behind to loved ones and earn a small picture of our face in the newspaper?
> There has to be more!
> Why am I here?
> How will I be remembered?
> What do I want told about my life?

By dinnertime, he completed his homework for Coach Erikson by crafting his 'Y.' It was much, much bigger than himself. Starting with the end in mind, Christian wrote a phrase that would be Why he wakes up every day, and he could not wait to share it with Coach next Monday.

The Freshman

18

Big Rocks

"Tristan, I'm heading to the library if you want to come," Christian offered from their dorm room on Sunday afternoon.

Tristan snickered with surprise and replied, "Library? We have one of those?"

Christian headed out the door alone and walked to the library listening to upbeat, positive music on his phone. He was still disappointed not to be with his family after his grandpa's funeral, but the lyrics and fresh air lifted his spirit as he walked. The library was surprisingly the most quiet, empty place on campus. Christian thought that at an academic institution there would be more students actually studying.

Getting back on the team was essential, and getting all A's and B's was central to the path back on the team. There was no way to erase his low scores from his lazy start. His actions held consequences, but he was not beating himself up over his past. He was looking forward to reaching his goals in the future.

The Freshman

He arrived at his Monday meeting with Coach wearing a clean, light-blue collared shirt and a nice pair of jeans.

Impressed, Coach stated, "You're looking sharp today, Christian. What's the occasion?"

"Nothing really," Christian replied.

"Well, when you dress like a professional, you will act like a professional." It wasn't long before their conversation led them back into their mentoring discussions. Christian shared his purpose—his Why—with Coach.

"Powerful!" exclaimed Coach Erikson. "I am so proud of you. You are overcoming adversity, consistently disconnecting, and now you answered your Why. Christian, you are killing it! I think you're ready for the 4th lesson of a comeback." He quieted his voice, almost down to a whisper. "This lesson holds tremendous value. If you make it part of your daily rhythms, it will change your life. Ready to hear it?"

Christian was intrigued and said, "Heck yeah!"

Coach Erikson grabbed a pen from his organized desk and a scratch piece of paper. On it, he drew a glass jar, sand, three big rocks, and some small pebbles:

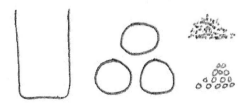

The Freshman

"Here is your task. You must fit all three of these items inside this glass jar. How do you get them all inside?" Coach Erikson asked.

"Let me think about it." Christian felt pressure to get this right as Coach Erikson handed him the pen.

"I think I got it," Christian said as he moved toward the desk. "The biggest ones will have to go in first." He began to draw the three big rocks inside the jar:

Followed by the small pebbles, and lastly the sand slipping through the gaps:

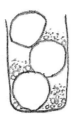

"Yes! You **Get Your BIG ROCKS In First!**" Coach said emphatically. Then he asked, "What are your Big Rocks?

"What do you mean by *Big Rocks*?" Christian asked as he tilted his head to the side.

"Your Big Rocks represent the three top priorities in your life. Now that you know your *Why*, we can focus on *What* we will be doing each day. The problem is this: small things creep in and distract us from the important things. First you have to decide what your three Big Rocks are," Coach stated as he held up three fingers.

"The number *three* is essential. We cannot fully concentrate on ten or even five big tasks. You have to know your three Big Rocks. What are yours? What do *you* have to do each day?" Coach Erikson asked with passion.

"I would say," Christian said as he closed his eyes to think hard, "My faith, my academics, and basketball. Those are my three Big Rocks right now."

They discussed Christian's Big Rocks and small pebbles before Christian began to list the sand. These were the wasteful, empty, and meaningless kinds of activities that steal away from top priorities.

"Social media, reality TV, video games . . ." Christian stopped even though he knew he had more time-wasters in his life.

"Perfect," Coach Erikson replied. Then he stared Christian straight in the eye and continued, "Listen here. The problem comes when we look back at the end of a day and see that all of the sand and pebbles got in, but we forgot one of the Big Rocks. Instead, I want you to learn to **Get Your BIG ROCKS In First**. My favorite teacher from high school always told me, 'Schedule time to schedule time.' That means every week, I have a set time where I sit down with my calendar, and I plan out the next two weeks."

Coach pointed to the picture of the glass jar and said, "Each day, I try to get my Big Rocks in first. If there is extra time, then I am free to chase extras *after* the Big Rocks are accomplished. Get it?"

Christian wrote this down in his Journal so he wouldn't forget.

> 1. Discover Who You Are Created to Be
> 2. Choose Right People
> 3. Listen and Learn from Everyone
> 4. Overcome Adversity
> 5. Consistently Disconnect to Question, Think, & Write
> 6. Live for a Y Bigger than u
> 7. Get Your BIG ROCKS in First

Coach continued, "Everyone says the biggest lesson students need to learn when they get to college is how to what . . . ? Manage their *time*. Time Management. But time management is a myth. Time continues to pass. You cannot control it, but you can control your priorities. You turn into a Priority Manager. That is what we are doing each and every day. Week after week for the rest of our lives. We are controlling priorities."

Nearing the end of their discussion, Coach Erikson concluded, "First you named your Big Rocks. Now the tough job is executing the plan every day—*every* single day for the rest of your life. Your homework is to write down your three Big Rocks for each day. And, I want you to fill out this time log to learn where you are spending your time."

Christian looked at the piece of paper that had an empty block for every hour of the week. "Yes sir," he said interested.

"Next Monday is my wife's birthday, and I am going to take her into the city to celebrate. Let's skip next week and meet back up the following. Midterms will be complete by then so we will know more about your future with the team at our next meeting. Deal?" Coach asked as he reached out to shake hands.

Christian shook Coach's hand and coached himself as he left the office, the next two weeks are crucial. If I focus on my Big Rocks, I can get back on the team.

19

Midterms

The stress levels were high. Next week was midterms, and the freshmen were not sure what to expect. What happened to my quiet table in the library? Christian wondered as he looked around estimating four times as many people were there today compared to last week. He found an empty room on the third floor where he took out his books, notes, daily planner, and time log that Coach gave him at their last meeting.

Completing the time log, Christian could see that he needed more sleep and that he wasn't spending as much time studying as he thought. He flipped to today's date in his planner to write down his Big Rocks for the day and to schedule out the week. He had his first midterm exam on Tuesday, another on Thursday, and three midterms on Friday.

On top of the stress from his academics, Tristan was announced as the 5th starter for the team's first scrimmage. It stung. Christian used to be the star in high school, and he wanted to get back on the team to show Coach that he could perform, too. That is why he had to ace these midterms.

Even with late nights, long study sessions, and the pressure of taking exams, Christian made it through the week. The midterms were taken. He had given his best. Monday's meeting with Coach would reveal the outcome.

20

Completing the Comeback

Christian's mind was a battlefield. He warred the fear of not making the grades as he walked nervously toward the meeting that would determine his future.

Quietly, he sat down across from Coach in the office. This office and the comfy couch he sat on had become one of his favorite places on campus.

Coach Erikson began speaking, "Christian, I am going to tell you straight. You did not meet the goal of getting all A's and B's after midterms."

Christian's heart sank. His head dropped, and he caught it with his hands. I worked my tail off. How could this be? he asked himself. He tried to compose himself quickly, lifting his eyes back to Coach.

"So," Coach Erikson continued delivering the bad news, "You still can't participate with the team this semester. You did pretty well earning three B's, but you still have a D in Biology and Psychology. I am really sorry to have to break the news to you because I know how hard you worked and how much this means to you."

"I can't believe it," Christian mumbled, trying to trap the tears in his eyes while a few escaped. "Can I join the team in January?"

"For sure. You will have to get all A's and B's for your final grades. Christian, the comeback is not complete yet so don't slack off now. I believe you can do it." Coach Erikson knew to never waste a crisis. "This setback leads in perfectly to the 5th and final step in *Making a Comeback*. It is the number one predictor of success in life. Any guesses?"

"Fight? Perseverance?" Christian guessed not feeling like fighting at the moment.

"That's right! I like to say it like this: you must **Grow Your Grit Muscle.** Grit is like a muscle. The more you work it out, the stronger it becomes. It doesn't matter what preschool you went to. What college. Wealth. Height. Appearance. Skin color or family name. The best way to know if someone will be a success is if they have *grit*. Read the definition on the page."

Christian turned to the correct page of *Making a Comeback* and began reading:

> Passion and perseverance for very long-term goals. Grit is having stamina. Grit is sticking with your future day in day out, not just for the week, not just for the month, but for years. And working really hard to make that future a reality. Grit is living life like it's a marathon, not a sprint.[1]

"Can we keep going in the midst of challenges and setbacks? And will we come out stronger after going through them?" Coach Erikson asked. "*Making a*

The Freshman

Comeback begins with the initial decision to **Overcome Adversity** and finishes with **Grow your Grit Muscle**."

Christian realized he never had this kind of grit before college, but he felt it growing from everything he had faced so far this semester.

"Let me illustrate one way to grow your grit muscle. Think about things that you are comfortable with. I would guess: living at home, competing in your high school gym, or maybe certain subjects in school. These are things that are so familiar to you. All of that is in this small box." Coach Erikson drew a small box on his white board with the words "Comfort Zone" in it.

"The Discomfort Zone is just like it sounds, and it is this space just beyond where you are comfortable. Some examples might be going into a new environment, having to make new friends, competing at a higher level, or attempting a difficult subject or task. Can you think of anything in yours?"

The Freshman

"You can grow grit," Coach Erikson continued, "by pursuing challenges in your Discomfort Zone. When you attempt the things in that space, there are two options. You *could* fail. But it's not *really* failing because you learn for the next challenge and your grit muscle grows just from trying. Or you *could* win. Then your grit muscle grows from seeing yourself succeed at something that was in your Discomfort Zone, and guess what? Your Comfort Zone then expands as you become more confident to take on bigger challenges."

The Freshman

"Look at all these students," Coach Erikson said as he pointed out the window at the students walking around campus. "Too many people are afraid to fail. They won't even try something new or difficult if they aren't 100% sure they will win, but today, *you* are the one with a choice. What are you going to do?"

"Coach, I can't quit now. I need that scholarship and really want to have a strong grit muscle."

"That's what I love to hear," Coach said. "Now you know all five steps to *Making a Comeback*. Moving forward, I am available if you ever need anything, and I'll check in with you every week through a text or a call. Then after we get your final grades, I will let you know if you can rejoin the team."

After thanking his coach and saying goodbye, Christian left the office and walked to his dorm room where he wrote in his Green Journal:

1. Discover Who You Are Created to Be
2. Choose Right People
3. Listen and Learn from Everyone
4. Overcome Adversity
5. Consistently Disconnect to Question, Think, & Write
6. Live for a Y Bigger than u
7. Get Your BIG ROCKS in First
8. Grow Your Grit Muscle

The Freshman

21

The Middle

The middle was not easy. The newness of college was beginning to fade, and the end line was not in sight.

While hanging out in their dorm room, Tristan asked, "Did you hear about the two guys from down the hall?"

Christian had heard that both of them left school—one quit because college was too hard and the other got kicked out for getting caught with drugs.

How far down the path could I have gone if I hadn't found who I was created to be? Christian thought. He saw many students on campus trying to fill the void in their lives with achievements, applause of others, drugs, or alcohol. He knew that none of these could fill the emptiness in their hearts. He found what they were looking for. Or it found him. He knew he was given the greatest gift—grace. A second chance, and he wanted to give his utmost to make the most of his life story. He told himself everyday: **Overcome the Adversity. Grow Your Grit Muscle.** Eight more weeks to finish strong.

The Freshman

22

Mom

The trees on campus were beginning to change with the onset of fall. Christian was mesmerized with God's creation. When outside, he would always look up to the sky, stars, or mountains and marvel at the beauty surrounding him.

"I'll catch up with you. I've got to pick up this call," Christian said to his friends. They were walking to the student union to play ping pong, but Christian hadn't talked to his mom for a couple of weeks. He wasn't the greatest at keeping in touch with his family. Last Christmas, Christian gave his mom a coupon as a gift. It read, "One Year of Answering the Phone Every Time You Call," and she loved it, even though he had missed a few of her calls.

Christian happily answered the phone, "Hey Mom!"

"My long-lost son. How is college treating you?" she asked.

"I am really enjoying life right now!"

"Great! I am proud of you, Chris." His mom had been calling him *Chris* since Kindergarten when his school friends began using Chris for short. He didn't want to share about his decision to be called 'Christian' yet because he wasn't sure how they would respond. He figured he would talk to them about it in person one day soon. She continued, "How is Coach Erikson? I just love that guy."

"He's good! I am still not back on the team, but he has met with me for four mentoring sessions and taught me some great lessons. We aren't meeting as much right now, but I am extremely grateful for him investing in me," Christian's attention was suddenly caught by the array of colors in the sunset.

"I have to say, Chris, you have been so fortunate to have role models like Coach Erikson." Christian was half listening and wondered if the sunset was more orange or red. His mom continued, "If you aren't formally meeting with Coach right now, you should **Seek A Mentor**. We all need 'a brain to pick, an ear to listen, and a push in the right direction.'[1] I don't know if you want to hear advice from your mom anymore, but once a mom, always a mom."

As soon as the words **"Seek a Mentor"** came across the phone, Christian's attention was drawn back to his conversation with his mom. This is the next step in my freshman journey, he thought. Immediately, he pulled out his Green Journal from his backpack. He takes it everywhere now because lessons were finding him left and right. This time, it even came from his mom. As she continued to tell him what his siblings were up to, he wrote:

> 1. Discover Who You Are Created to Be
> 2. Choose Right People
> 3. Listen and Learn from Everyone
> 4. Overcome Adversity
> 5. Consistenty Disconnect to Question, Think, & Write
> 6. Live for a Y Bigger than u
> 7. Get Your BIG ROCKS in First
> 8. Grow Your Grit Muscle
> 9. Seek a Mentor

He gave a few "uh huhs" and "sounds goods" before his mom asked the last question, "Anyone in mind to be your mentor?"

Christian knew exactly who he wanted.

The Freshman

23

The Mentor

Christian had an open invitation to get a meal with Andre—the senior captain of the football team. Asking Andre was definitely in Christian's Discomfort Zone, but Christian decided to find Andre and seek him as a mentor.

He gave a light knock on Andre's door before entering and tapping Andre on the shoulder. Wearing headphones while studying with his back to the door, Andre jumped up and said, "Dude! You scared me!" He took his headphones off, smiled, and continued, "I am so pumped to see you though. Whatcha been up to?"

Christian didn't know how to ask Andre to be his mentor, but after a few minutes of talking in circles, Christian spit out the words, "I'm also trying to learn from strong leaders, so I came to see if I can buy you a meal and ask you some questions."

"Heck yeah! Let's go get some food, but you don't have to pay for me. Two minutes, and I'll be ready." Andre closed his laptop and marked the page in his textbook. Then he put on his shoes and grabbed a flat-billed hat that he liked to wear backwards.

Christian and Andre went down the stairs and out to the parking lot before jumping in Andre's Jeep. They got to know each other a little better while eating pizza and talking about sports, girls, and the future. The only thing that Christian did not like was Andre's choice of country music playing while they drove back to campus.

From the student parking lot, they walked briskly as temperatures were dropping, and Andre inquired, "What are you doing this Saturday?"

"No plans," Christian answered. "What's going on?"

"One lesson I learned freshman year is that if you are going to **Choose Right People**, you have to **Choose Right Places**."

"What do you mean, right places?" Christian asked.

"Too many people say they want to surround themselves with quality, caring friends, but every week, they go to the wrong places. My freshman year, I found the greatest friends at CampusServe where we met at 10 am on Saturdays to serve at a youth center. When my team doesn't have a game, I get to go. There are two groups. One walks the neighborhood to find kids who want to play sports at the center. The second finds families who need work done around the house."

Christian could tell that this place meant a lot to Andre.

"Seeing the smile on the kid's faces," Andre continued. "It's priceless. Most college students are sleeping in after a rough Friday night, but this group shows up every week to simply serve. Football is off this Saturday if you want to try it out. And who knows? Maybe you will find your future Mrs. there."

"I'm in. **Choose Right Places**. And if a find a potential date there, icing on the cake," Christian said with a grin.

"Alright, CampusServe Saturday. And Mexican Night is next Tuesday. Buy a burrito, get one free. We can continue our chat there," Andre said as he clapped it up with Christian.

"Sounds good. Thanks so much," Christian said as he went into his dorm room where Tristan was playing video games alone.

"Ah, the life of a college student," Christian stated. "How are your classes going? Gonna be eligible next semester?"

"You know. Doing what I need to do so I can keep playing ball," Tristan replied.

Christian sat on his bed and thought about Tristan and Andre. Both were amazing athletes but their habits, character, and relationships revealed glaring differences. Andre was coming into the inner circle. Tristan was drifting out. **Choose Right People**, Christian thought.

The momentum of the lessons was building, and it was becoming easier after each positive choice—like a skier heading downhill. The power was not merely in learning these lessons. The power came from applying them immediately. They became a part of his DNA—who he was. He was not perfect, no one is. But he was striving for his best and growing every day.

The Freshman

Christian added the lesson to his Green Journal:

> 1. Discover Who You Are Created to Be
> 2. Choose Right People
> 3. Listen and Learn from Everyone
> 4. Overcome Adversity
> 5. Consistently Disconnect to Question, Think, & Write
> 6. Live for a Y Bigger than u
> 7. Get Your BIG ROCKS in First
> 8. Grow Your Grit Muscle
> 9. Seek a Mentor
> 10. Choose Right Places

He was confident he could make all A's and B's to get back on the team, but even if the deal with Coach falls through, he knew he was on the path to acing this semester of his life.

24

The Weekend

Four games into the season, Tristan was leading the team in scoring as Christian watched every home game from the stands. Christian had always lived for game days. I should be out there, he told himself. This Friday night, a Top 25 team was in town, and the crowd, cheerleaders, and band made the gym the place to be on campus.

Christian had met about twelve other "right people" from Andre's circle, and they all sat together in the front row of the student section. As time expired, Tristan hit the game winner, and just about all the students rushed the floor putting Tristan on their shoulders as the hero. From the stands, Christian clapped as he imagined being the hero for this school one day.

While exiting the gym, Christian passed by Tristan who was being congratulated by a group of mostly girls. Tristan stepped away for a minute and whispered, "Hey man, want to hit up the after party?"

Choose Right Places, Christian thought immediately and respectfully declined Tristan's invitation.

Christian and his new friends created their own kind of fun that evening. They played games in the student rec center and went out for a late-night meal.

The next morning, Christian and his friends met at CampusServe where Christian played basketball with six younger boys at a youth center. "Come on, you gotta be quick," Christian encouraged them as they tried to steal the ball. They adored him, and he walked away surprisingly fulfilled.

Driving back to campus, Andre invited Christian to a Sunday morning gathering. Christian decided to continue to **Choose Right Places**. "One hundred percent, I'll be there," he answered.

His soul was filling up. Up to this point in Christian's life, all of his relationships had been self-centered. What could he get his parents to buy him? Did his girlfriend make him more popular? But now his heart was changing into a person who came to serve rather than be served. Who can I encourage? Who needs love today? God was transforming him, and a positive peer pressure was pushing Christian toward better things.

Thanksgiving break was a few weeks away, and Christian's car was still not fixed. Knowing this, Andre asked, "Want to come to my house for the break? My parents are cool with it if you want to."

The offer caught Christian off guard. "Really? Man,

that is super generous. Umm . . . Let me think about it."

"Just let me know. I have a big family, and they are used to extra people being around."

Christian thanked Andre and told him he would let him know soon. He walked out of Andre's room and started down the hallway. **Choose Right Places** popped in his head again. Christian quickly turned around and shouted into Andre's room, "Dude, I don't want to be a burden, but I would love to come."

"Let's go!" Andre roared. "Road trip!"

The Freshman

The Freshman

25

Thanksgiving Break

Christian threw a small bag of clothes and his book bag into Andre's SUV. The book bag contained his Green Journal and Book he tried to read each day. Then Christian rode off with Andre and two of Andre's friends six hours north to their hometown.

Christian had plenty of time in the car to think, talk, and listen to music. Recently, he had been trying to figure out what major would lead him to the perfect career. He had found his identity, purpose, and daily priorities, but he was struggling with not knowing his future or having an answer to the question, "What is the vision for my life?" The weeks behind were full of life and meaning, and he could foresee accomplishing his goals for the next semester, but what about a vision for five or ten years out? It was overwhelming for Christian to plan that far ahead.

Scrolling through social media while riding shotgun, he saw a quote that spoke to him. "Big Time is where you're at."[1] Then minutes later, he read, "If it's not God's time, you can't force it. When it is God's time, you can't stop it."² He realized that when it is the *right time*, he would know what to do. Until then, he would be faithful with what he had. Worrying about the years ahead would not help. He knew what he had today. Big Time is where you're at, Christian told himself.

The friends arrived at Andre's parents' house as the sun set in the suburban neighborhood. It was a nice-sized two-story house with a basement and gray siding. Andre had four younger siblings, and his parents brought their 21 year-old nephew to live with them to get his life back on track. They must have a massive washer and dryer, Christian thought.

Christian was used to a quiet house, but after a few days with Andre's family, he was drawn to the love and energy in their home. They were always competing in board games, card games, and sports, and the TV was only turned on once to watch a movie in the evening. They sat down at the dinner table together to pray and enjoy a home-cooked meal.

Christian saw Andre's father respond with quiet strength, no matter the situation. The rebelling of a high school boy or the immaturity of a 9 year-old girl could not get Andre's dad to lose his cool. This is the type of man I want to be when I grow up, Christian thought.

One evening after dinner, he had an opportunity to talk with Andre's dad. Christian wanted to **Listen and Learn from Everyone**, especially from a man full of wisdom, so he asked thoughtful questions like: How did you meet your wife? Why did you select your career? What made you stand out compared to your peers? Did you picture life playing out the way it did? Christian would never forget the response to that question. Andre's dad said, "Your life is like a book. You can make predictions about what will happen later in the story based off the book cover or title. Once you begin reading, you can guess what will happen in the next chapter, but you never know what will happen next until you read *that* page."

The week was flying by. Andre's family helped serve Thanksgiving meals to struggling families. Every other day, Andre, his brothers, and Christian lifted weights in the basement, and most days Christian worked to improve his basketball game by going to the local high school with Andre's brother.

Christian learned a lot from the trip. He noticed how Andre's father was affectionate to his wife and kids, and how even the guys were not afraid to say "I love you" to each other. Additionally, the children actually respected their parents by showing honor and appreciation for things like home-cooked meals, clean clothes, and time spent together.

Christian couldn't remember where he heard the quote, but it came to him after watching Andre with his family, "A turtle on a fence post did not get there by himself." Christian saw Andre standing high as a leader, and he realized Andre's upbringing played a major role. He remembered that Andre called his dad multiple times each week to stay connected, and he witnessed a spirit of gratitude within their family.

The crew returned to campus, and Christian unpacked his clothes and took out his Green Journal from his book bag. He had realized on the drive home that he learned his next lesson, but this time it was not spoken. Christian witnessed this from Andre's family:

> 1. Discover Who You Are Created to Be
> 2. Choose Right People
> 3. Listen and Learn from Everyone
> 4. Overcome Adversity
> 5. Consistently Disconnect to Question, Think, & Write
> 6. Live for a Y Bigger than u
> 7. Get Your BIG ROCKS in First
> 8. Grow Your Grit Muscle
> 9. Seek a Mentor
> 10. Choose Right Places
> 11. Express Gratitude to Loved Ones

He asked himself, who has impacted me to become who I am today? Who should I be thankful for?

He wrote one thank you note, followed by another. After nearly twenty minutes, he had written letters to his high school coach, his parents, Coach Erikson, and Andre.

He set down his pen, looked out the window, and took a deep breath in and exhaled slowly. Now it was back to the grind. Finals were approaching, and the weight of getting back on the team was like a piano on his back.

26

Final Grades

With his car fixed and first semester complete, Christian arrived at his mom's house safely. He rushed inside, leaving his caffeine and trash in the car. "Hey! Chris is home!" his mom yelled as his smiling siblings ran to greet him before he could get past the entryway. "I missed you guys this semester," Christian confessed while giving his younger brother and sister a hug.

He grabbed his belongings and took them to his room. "The glory days," Christian said as he looked around at old trophies and pictures. Christian went back downstairs to be with his family and kicked back in his favorite recliner. After checking his grades on his phone, he bragged to his mom, "Genius in the house!" Three A's were posted so far, but he was still waiting for his final exams to post in Biology and Psychology—the two classes with D's at midterms. Depending on the test scores, his grades could fall as low as a C, but he would know for certain his position on the team within days.

Christian spent time at both of his parents' houses

and was able to see most of his old friends. After one semester, he had grown so much from his mistakes, lessons, and setbacks, but he was surprised to see that most of his friends hadn't changed at all—or at least as far as he could tell. This made Christian oddly appreciative for all that he had faced.

One afternoon, Christian stopped by Ashley's house to discuss their past relationship and thoughts on their future. After a thirty-minute conversation standing in her driveway, they both decided that getting back together was not in their cards. Despite having some feelings for his high school sweetheart, Christian believed getting back together would be like taking a step back rather than progressing forward—where his lessons were taking him.

After an awkward goodbye hug, he got in his car and sighed. He believed that God had someone out there for him to date and marry one day. For now, he wanted to become the kind of guy who would attract the right kind of girl.

Before exiting Ashley's circle driveway, his phone dinged. It was a text from Coach:

The Freshman

Christian's adrenaline was rushing. Did I make the grades?

He logged in with his phone to view his grades and saw that he made one B and the rest A's, finishing on the Dean's List in his first semester.

"Vamos!" Christian yelled in Spanish as he fist-pumped to celebrate. He had picked up a few new phrases from the international guys on his hall. Christian called his dad as he drove and shared the news with his mom when he arrived home.

Later that night, he received another message from Coach:

The Freshman

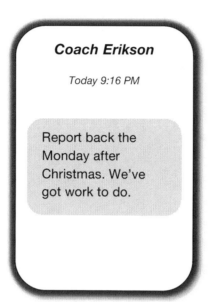

It was like a dream. He was back on the team! He had pictured this day, and then he worked all semester toward this goal. Now he was one step closer to earning his scholarship.

27

Christmas Break

Christian's focus intensified after learning that he was back on the team. He went to his high school gym every day of the break to practice and lift because he did not want to ride the bench. He wanted to be an impact player—even as a freshman.

Outside of his time at the gym, Christian had great conversations and good times over the break. He hugged his mom a little extra and even built up the courage to tell his family about discovering who he was created to be and being called 'Christian' now. He showed his dad all the lessons he learned in one semester, took his teenage sister to get her favorite ice cream, and played video games with his little brother. "Make *every* day a masterpiece because every day is a gift. Every day is a blessing," Christian reminded them and tried to live by.

By the end of the break, Christian was itching to go back to his college. One full semester and his college campus felt like home, like it was where he belonged. It wasn't just the physical structures but the solid relationships that he had built. Christian needed to visit home to close the door on his past. He was able to see firsthand that his family had adjusted to life without him and his old friends had made new friends. Now there was nothing holding him back from the semester ahead.

After telling his family he loved them, Christian packed his car, entered the address to pull up the directions on his phone, and drove away. He had one semester to make an impact and—hopefully—earn a scholarship for next year.

28

Weights

Christian began his quest to gain trust and earn playing time the second he got back to campus. He spent hours watching game film and studying the team's offense to try to make up for the months of missed practice. I know all of our plays, but I need playing time to fully get my game back, he thought.

Christian was grateful that he was able to travel to two away games early in January, but he didn't play in either game. The season was spiraling as the team lost both games and dropped to 7th place in the conference standings. Christian wanted to help the team win, but he was lacking a niche, a specialty that his coaches could call on.

With a week before their next game, the team was able to get a couple extra lifts in. Christian had built a good relationship with his Strength Coach, Jack, who was in his late twenties and worked as an assistant under the long-time Head Strength Coach. Christian was not sure if Jack was his real name or a nickname, but either way, it was fitting because the guy was jacked. The team knew that fitness, nutrition, and health were important to Jack, which gave him instant respect and credibility.

Since Christian didn't have class for a few hours, he leisurely stretched after a morning lift. Also, he was stalling because he had a few questions for Jack. He found Jack setting up for the next team to work out and asked, "I have been watching you this semester, and I love how you lead our team with energy and passion. Where does your passion come from?"

"Well, I have decided to give my all no matter where I am. Even when no one is watching, I want to serve in the shadows," Jack answered in the dimly lit basement weight room that was in need of some upgrades.

Christian had another question on his mind, "The Head Strength Coach is nearing retirement. Are you working hard so that you can get that promotion?"

"A couple years ago, I would have said yes. I was dreaming of progressing and thought I was ready for that position. But man, I still had so much to learn. So I changed my perspective," Jack paused as he took a drink from his water bottle. "'Be so good they can't ignore you.'[1] My mindset each day is to do good work. If I can do that every day while caring for people, then the promotions, positions, and pay will find me."

"I love that. Last question," Christian said before asking the question that he really wanted to ask, "I have been trying to earn a scholarship and get playing time. Do you have any advice? Any at all?"

"**Give your All—and Then Some**," Jack said without hesitation. "There is no secret sauce to success. You just have to grind, outwork the competition, and find that little extra that no one else is willing to do. This is how you will separate yourself and rise to the top. **Give your All—and Then Some.** I see your sweat equity in our weight training sessions. Is this the way you play basketball?" Jack asked.

"Honestly, no." Christian admitted. "I am struggling to catch Coach's eye. There is at least one guy on the team who has more skill than me. Scoring, passing, rebounding, defending. Even if I give my all and then some, it will be tough to pass them." Christian paused. Then he asked with desperation, "How do you catch people ahead of you?"

"Hustle. Is there a guy on the team known for his hustle? Do the dirty work. Grind. Scrap. Every day. In the shadows at practice or when the lights turn on for a big game, be the guy that inspires others by giving your all. Every team needs *that* kind of guy," Jack said as he hit his chest with his fist. "One who will sacrifice his body for others."

"It's worth a try. I'll try to be that guy," Christian said not sure what the result would be. Then he packed his bag with his wallet and keys and walked out of the weight room. Noticing his shirt was drenched, full of sweat, he thought with pride, **Give your All—and Then Some.**

That afternoon at practice, Christian gave his everything on the court and held nothing back—sprinting, diving, and sweating all over the hardwood floor. Coach Erikson noticed his extra hustle and asked Christian, "Where did this relentless effort come from?"

"I'm going to give my all and then some for the rest of the season, Coach," Christian answered.

At the end of practice, Coach Erikson addressed the team. "Christian laid it all on the line today. Can anyone question his desire to play in our next game? Listen," he scanned every player in the huddle to see if they were making eye contact. "Listen to me. I need your eyes. We aren't reaching our potential because not everyone is giving their all. Team-first wins! **Give Your All—And Then Some**—for the *team*. This is how we will turn our season around." Coach walked out of the gym after this statement, and a few seconds later the players walked slowly away from the huddle.

After showering back at his dorm, Christian found his Green Journal and wrote the newest lesson that he learned from Jack:

The Freshman

1. Discover Who You Are Created to Be
2. Choose Right People
3. Listen and Learn from Everyone
4. Overcome Adversity
5. Consistently Disconnect to Question, Think, & Write
6. Live for a Y Bigger than u
7. Get Your BIG ROCKS in First
8. Grow Your Grit Muscle
9. Seek a Mentor
10. Choose Right Places
11. Express Gratitude to Loved Ones
12. Give Your All—And Then Some

The Freshman

29

What Else?

"How is your day going?" Coach Erikson asked Christian as they walked toward the gym on a bright but chilly winter day.

"I'm giving my all today, Coach," Christian replied before opening the door for his Coach.

Christian was off to an exceptional start this semester with straight A's and off-the-charts hustle every day at practice. His body was continuously sore from pushing it past what was normal, but he enjoyed that feeling now. The extreme hustle was contagious, and Coach Erikson starting giving Christian some playing time and used his energy as a spark whenever the team went flat. Christian's stats weren't glamorous, but his hustle helped advance his team up to 3rd place in their conference.

Coach and Christian walked and talked together down to the basement of the basketball gym. They split directions as Coach headed for his office and Christian entered the weight room.

After the morning lift, Christian was on the floor working out some soreness with a foam roller. Lying on his side, he saw Jack walk by and asked, "Hey, Jack, can we talk?" Jack listened to Christian share about his frustration with not performing better in the games.

"I love your drive, but be patient," Jack said realizing that Christian needed encouragement. "You sat out for an entire semester. You'll get it back. You're hustling and giving your all, and that is why Coach is playing you. Plus, your extra effort motivates the team and is helping you guys win."

"It's not easy to be patient," Christian replied. "I want quicker results. What else can I do to get back to my peak performance?"

"There is one thing I have seen work for others. Are you sure you want to hear it?" Jack asked. Christian nodded and leaned toward Jack, ready to learn another lesson.

"Fuel Your High-Performance Sports Car," Jack stated.

With a look of confusion, Christian asked, "A sports car? Have you seen my old car? It barely runs."

"Your High-Performance Sports Car is your body. Some sports cars can cost upwards of $500,000. Plus, to maintain it, there are so many added costs after purchasing." Jack found the most beautiful sports car on his phone and showed Christian the picture. "Extra taxes, super high insurance, crazy costs for replacement parts, and the ridiculous costs to maintain it. For example, an oil change for an F355 Ferrari is $1,100[1] and you have to use premium fuel every fill up."

"What does any of that have to do with me?"

The Freshman

Christian asked.

"Your body is worth *more* than that high-performance car. If you make $40,000 a year, it would only take you 12.5 years to earn half a million dollars. Sadly, we treat our nice cars with luxury treatment while feeding our bodies junk. What did you eat today? . . . Anything good?"

Christian could not think of one healthy food he had eaten that day. Jack continued, "Over one third of American adults eat fast food every day,[2] and just 1 in 10 adults eat adequate fruits and vegetables.[3] Our health is declining, and I believe that what you feed your body will impact everything you do."

Christian considered his diet and began speaking, "I have never eaten well, but I am active. I burn whatever I eat."

"So many athletes think this way, but you are wrong. What you put in your body matters. It could be the edge you are looking for. What if you put lemonade or soda in the gas tank of your car? Maybe it would run for a block, but it will kill your car eventually because it needs the right kind of fuel. Just like your body. Hear this," Jack pounded his fist into his palm. "Two hundred years ago, the average American ate only 2 pounds of sugar a year. Today, the average American consumes almost 152 pounds of sugar in one year. This is 3 pounds of sugar consumed in one week!"[4]

"That is insane. I do love the cookies in the cafeteria. I get one after every dinner," Christian admitted.

"And it's not only food. Think about the music, social media, movies, or shows you consume. Think about your sleep. All of these feed your body and mind, playing a major role in how strong you are. I want you to become the expert of health, nutrition, and what you put in your body. It's not about your size, weight, or image. It's about *life* and health. Being a strong instrument for God to use for many years," Jack said as he flexed his bicep.

It would be nice to look like Jack, Christian thought.

Jack continued, "Let's start basic. Write down everything you eat and drink for a week. Bring it back to me next week, and then we will go from there. Got it?"

Christian left the conversation inspired to improve his health, and when he arrived back to his now familiar dorm, he grabbed his Green Journal. He didn't learn a major lesson every day, but he was always listening and learning. Today he wrote down his 13th lesson of his freshman year.

1. Discover Who You Are Created to Be
2. Choose Right People
3. Listen and Learn from Everyone
4. Overcome Adversity
5. Consistently Disconnect to Question, Think, & Write
6. Live for a Y Bigger than u
7. Get Your BIG ROCKS in First
8. Grow Your Grit Muscle
9. Seek a Mentor
10. Choose Right Places
11. Express Gratitude to Loved Ones
12. Give Your All - And Then Some
13. Fuel Your High-Performance Sports Car

The Freshman

30

Discipline

"Ninety-eight, ninety-nine, one hundred. Boom!" Christian shouted after finishing his 100 pushups to start the day. Standing to his feet without a shirt on, he stared at the picture of the high-performance sports car that he hung on the wall of his dorm room. He stationed himself in front of the mirror and thought, not bad. Making progress.

He was now disciplining himself in every way. His spiritual life, relationships, work, finances, and health were all thriving. Spiritually, he continued to wake up early—almost every morning to disconnect from the noise of the world and connect with God. He was striving to be the best son, brother, friend, and teammate he could be. For Christian, his work was done in the classroom and on the basketball court. Financially, he lived on a budget, telling his money where to go rather than wondering where it went,[1] and Christian was learning how to be more generous—even with the little that he did have as a broke college student. He realized that he was not the owner of his money, but a money manager for the real Owner.[2]

Now the final area to focus on was his health. He did not realize his diet was out of control. From writing down everything he ate for the week, he learned that he was clearly addicted to sugar and that every meal ended with something sweet. He also saw that he ate too much fast food and processed junk.

After researching the benefits of healthy eating for almost an hour in his room, Christian began to share his findings with Tristan.

"Did you know that eating healthy not only decreases the chances of getting all the major diseases like cancer, heart disease, stroke, and diabetes, but it can also improve your memory and mood? It can help you sleep better, too,"[3] Christian informed, as if he were a doctor.

"Ah, I see," Tristan said half listening and looking at his phone.

"Jack challenged me to try to go seven days without eating any added sugar. It will be tough, and I will probably get a headache after a couple of days. They say that sugar is more addictive than cocaine."[4]

Christian could tell that his roommate was disinterested. Then he began thinking about what he wanted to eat at the cafeteria for dinner with his new philosophy—eat what was created on the earth rather than what was made in a factory.

With his success and momentum building, Christian looked at the goal he had written on an index card and placed on his desk. He looked at it most nights before bed and visualized it happening. It read:

The Freshman

> Earn the Scholarship.
> Ace Your Life.

The Freshman

31

Motives

Christian survived the sugar withdrawal. He was surprised how powerful that ingredient was, but by the end of his detox, Christian was feeling better than ever. During the day, he had great energy, and at night, he slept like a baby.

His vital role on the team continued—the gritty guy doing the dirty work. His stats weren't showing, but the team kept winning. Coach Erikson was pleased with his players' extra effort at practice and in their daily habits. He knew this was a direct result of Christian giving his all and then some. More players were doing the small things well, and their culture went from doing what was required to doing that little extra that separates excellent from mediocre.

Everyone was buying in—except for Tristan. He was lighting up the stat sheet, but Coach Erikson and his teammates knew that eventually it would catch up to him. Coach Erikson always quoted, "Talent can get you to the top, but character will keep you there."[1]

The team was heading into the conference tournament as the #2 seed, and they had to win the 3-

game tournament to advance to Nationals. Christian had been told over and over that he was a hard worker and how much he helped the team. But he was frustrated by not playing more to showcase himself. Troubled, Christian wondered, what will I do next semester if I don't get this scholarship?

He entered his Coach's office to ask some questions about the conference tournament. He began, "I know we have a chance to be the first team to ever go to Nationals, and I don't want to distract you or the team from that goal. But I would like to hear your thoughts on how you will use me for this final tournament."

"The same way we have been playing. What we are doing is working."

Christian assumed this, but he just had to know for certain. Coach continued, "We are the hottest team in the nation, and you are responsible for that."

Christian's body language shrunk. "Yes sir. I respect that."

"Why do you want more playing time?" Coach asked noticing that Christian was upset.

"I think you know this, but my parents are not going to pay for the rest of my education. So I was hoping that if I played more, you would be more willing to offer me the scholarship to stay here next year," Christian replied.

"I see. I may have misread all your hustle and extra effort. I thought you were sacrificing your body for the team. But it looks like your **And Then Some** was all about you?" Coach asked.

Christian heard the disappointment in his voice

and sat without words.

"It's not about you," Coach Erikson said pointing at Christian. "Your skills and talents are not about you. **Serve YOUR Team**. You must change your reason for why you play. Look around. There are twelve other guys on this team that you can impact. They are your purpose. Remember? They are why you are here. It's not about you. **Serve YOUR Team!**"

"Yes sir," Christian said, feeling like he was caught committing a crime. He had heard Coach speak directly to the team before, but this felt different. Coach corrected Christian's selfishness with a firm, but still loving heart of a teacher.

"Christian, we tend to go through life dreaming of money, success, and personal gain. I wrestle with this daily, but those things only satisfy for a little while. They aren't eternal. If we only live and work so we can personally benefit, we've missed our purpose in life."

Christian stopped and thought about how he had worked extra for a scholarship and how the team did benefit some from it. But he knew his motive behind giving his all and fueling his body was not to serve the team—but self.

His reflection was interrupted as Coach continued, "Remember that *love* is the most powerful motivator in *all* the world. Let your love for others drive you to **Serve YOUR Team**. Mustering up enough energy will eventually run dry, but a heart full of Love will *never* run dry," Coach Erikson said. He spoke with so much emotion that Christian could see his eyes begin to well up.

Christian realized Coach served his players and the team as a whole with this kind of love. So Christian determined that he would also let love drive him and said to his Coach, "I'll **Serve YOUR Team**."

With that, Christian left Coach's office, went outside the gym, and noticed the trees budding and the fresh smell of spring. He grabbed his Green Journal and wrote down his next lesson:

1. Discover Who You Are Created to Be
2. Choose Right People
3. Listen and Learn from Everyone
4. Overcome Adversity
5. Consistently Disconnect to Question, Think, & Write
6. Live for a Y Bigger than u
7. Get Your BIG ROCKS in First
8. Grow Your Grit Muscle
9. Seek a Mentor
10. Choose Right Places
11. Express Gratitude to Loved Ones
12. Give Your All—And Then Some
13. Fuel Your High-Performance Sports Car
14. Serve YOUR Team

32

Scholarship

The team went on to win the conference tournament and advanced to Nationals for the first time in program history. Tristan scored 36 points, hit the game-winning basket, and earned the MVP of the conference championships. Christian served his team with a heart full of Love.

At the end of the season, Christian met with Coach to discuss the past season and future scholarship. Sadly, the university made a cut to the budgets of all athletic programs, and Coach Erikson could not offer Christian a scholarship. Coach felt horrible, and Christian was crushed.

At the start of the year, Christian was lost, lonely, and wanted to leave. But now he knew The Way, felt connected, and really wanted to stay.

After a few days to process the bad news, he decided he would **Overcome Adversity**, yet again, and he knew his grit muscle would grow through the process of finding a new school. Rather than dwelling on the past, he had to make a plan for the future. He spent the final weeks of the semester focusing on his classes and messaging other coaches to find a scholarship. Those were his Big Rocks.

After finals were complete, Christian had two days to move out of the dorms. He looked back on the fourteen lessons he wrote down in his Green Journal. What a wild ride it has been, he thought. But I have no clue where I will . . . Before he could finish his thought, his phone rang. It was from an unknown number. Usually, he would let it go to voicemail, but something inside him said, "Pick it up."

The conversation ended and Christian sat stunned. Out of nowhere, an opportunity found him. A leader within the university heard about Christian's freshman story and offered him a Resident Assistant (RA) position in the dorms. If he accepted it, he would get free room and board but would still have a hefty tuition bill to cover. Moments after hanging up, Coach Erikson messaged Christian to meet tomorrow at 10 am. Coach had a proposal.

33

Tristan

Later in the day, Tristan returned to the dorm after his meeting with Coach and told Christian, "A D1 school offered me a spot on their team. Their facility, budgets, and prestige, I have to go."

"But here, you get to be the star," Christian argued. "And you have a coach and teammates who care about you. You're the guy taking the shot at the end of the game. You might ride the bench like me at your new school," Christian joked.

"Nah, I will be the man there, too," Tristan said with assurance.

"How did your grades end up?" Christian asked. "Any issues with eligibility to transfer?"

Christian never saw Tristan studying, but Tristan answered, "I should be alright. We will find out soon."

With Tristan planning to leave, Coach Erikson now had an extra scholarship available.

The Freshman

34

Two Options

The next morning after breakfast, Christian checked his grades and felt proud after seeing them. Then he walked to the gym and entered Coach's office wondering if Tristan's transfer would change anything. Christian was full of Peace and ready to hear Coach's proposal. A few steps inside the door, Coach gave his normal welcome-to-the-office hug, sat in his black leather chair, and cut right to the deal.

"Two options for you," Coach Erikson began. "I want to offer you a manager's scholarship. I was made aware of the RA position you were offered, so together, they would combine to create a full scholarship for meals, housing, and tuition. You would work with me as a Student Assistant Coach mentoring the freshmen, and I would mentor you. There would be some dirty work done behind the scenes, but three years of this would prepare you for a career in coaching."

"Wow! Thanks so much, Coach," Christian said thankful for the chance to stay at his college but unsure about his playing career coming to an end. So he asked, "What about the other option? You said there were two?"

"Well, with Tristan leaving, I have an extra scholarship available. It was heavy on my heart, so I prayed hard last night. Then I realized that you did everything I asked. You made your comeback, aced this semester academically, and served *our* team. You earned this scholarship, and I would be proud for you to represent our team next year."

Christian did not take any time before responding, "Coach, you do not know how much this means to me! I worked all year for this. There were moments when I started to doubt, but I . . . I don't know what to say. I'll work all summer so I can lead this team back to Nationals next year."

Christian took the scholarship paper and left coach's office ecstatic.

Official Letter of Intent

Name: Christian   .
Sport: Men's Basketball   .
Scholarship: Full   .

He called his family to share the good news as he walked back to his dorm room. After the phone calls, he breathed in the smells and sights from the campus. Maybe next year I will be the star leading this team, he thought.

Almost back to his dorm, he reflected on the year. Sometimes these stories do not end well. Sometimes the team loses, relationships fade, or family members die. Christian felt blessed for the perfect ending to his Freshman Year story.

35

The Final Lesson

Christian climbed onto the bed of his dorm room for the very last time and thought about his Coach's impact. His Freshman Year—his entire life could have completely derailed, but his Coach entered his world. Coach reached out and cared for me the moment I needed it most, Christian thought.

Instantaneously, it was like someone whispered in his ear. Everything made sense. It was all clear now. He had a vision for his life. He knew what major to pick and where he wanted to invest his time. He jumped out of his bed, grabbed his laptop, and began typing an email. It read:

> Dear Coach Erikson,
>
> I want to say THANK YOU. You stepped in my Freshman Year when I needed help. I was completely lost and had no clue who I was or where I was going. You generously gave me your valuable time. The strength of your hugs and uplifting words showed me love. You helped guide me to my identity, purpose, and priorities. You taught

me about adversity and grit, and I am eternally grateful that you were my Coach.

I want to accept your offer to be your Student Assistant Coach. You can use my scholarship to recruit a future star. I want to serve this school as an RA to be there for freshmen when they show up to their new adventure. After I graduate, I want to coach so I can enter the lives of others and be a strong mentor—like you. I look forward to working closely with you.

I have been writing down every lesson I have learned from my Freshman Year, and I am determined to continue writing lessons down so I can write a book one day. I pray that my story can help others ace the next semester of their life.

My Best,
Christian

After sending the email, Christian wrote the final lesson from his freshman year in his Green Journal:

The Freshman

1. Discover Who You Are Created to Be
2. Choose Right People
3. Listen and Learn from Everyone
4. Overcome Adversity
5. Consistenty Disconnect to Question, Think, & Write
6. Live for a Y Bigger than u
7. Get Your BIG ROCKS in First
8. Grow Your Grit Muscle
9. Seek a Mentor
10. Choose Right Places
11. Express Gratitude to Loved Ones
12. Give Your All – And Then Some
13. Fuel Your High-Performance Sports Car
14. Serve YOUR Team
15. Multiply...

The Freshman

Epilogue

The Epilogue of this book is the life that you will live—the lessons that I have learned, multiplied into your life.

Please contact me if you want to hear more about the Way to ace your life—or if I can help you with anything else. I leave you with this:

> Find who you were
> created to be. Live for
> what will matter in 10,000 years.

Meet with the Father. Surround yourself with people who will spur you on toward eternal things. Prioritize your life & live the abundant life that is ready for you.

> Persevere through adversity.
> Breathe, then look around.
> Find someone to pour into.
> Teaching them to find Life
> and then to multiply.

Then your Epilogue and mine will be their life. Their story. And the lives they will touch. And on and on…

The Freshman

Your Next Step

Now what? Here are four "next steps" you could take:

1. Pick one lesson from this book that speaks to you and do the homework today.

2. Use this Action Plan as a 15-day challenge to discovering who you are created to be. If this speaks to you, start with Lesson 1 and do one lesson per day.

3. Buy *The Freshman Journal* to dig deeper and discover who you are created to be. It is a 15-week journal with bible verses, questions, and space to write. This is where I see the biggest changes and the deepest work being done.

4. Multiply to others by downloading the free PDF Team Bible Study to lead others through the lessons.
This can be found at coachchadsimpson.com.

Homework to Ace the Next Semester of Your Life

1. Discover Who You Are Created To Be

"Find something solid, unshakable. No matter how much success you have in life or if it all comes crashing down and you lose everything, who you really are—your identity—should remain the same."
–Chad Simpson

Big Question: Who am I?

Homework:

☐ **Download the YouVersion Bible App** on your phone. **Open the App** and read at least the verse of the day.

2. Choose Right People

"The fastest way to lose sight of your identity is by walking with the wrong crowd. Finding the right people for your inner circle is key." –Chad Simpson

Big Question: Who am I surrounding myself with?

Homework:

☐ **Analyze your friends**. Think about all of the people you interact with on a weekly basis. Then make three lists:

List 1- Write all of the people who you know would be a good friend.

> ➢ Make an effort to spend more time with these friends

List 2- Write all the names of the people you are confident are not the right friends

> ➢ Look to serve someone from List 2

List 3- Write all of the friends who you are unsure of.

> ➢ Be careful of these friends until you know if you can trust them in your inner circle or you know they are in your life so you can impact them.

3. Listen and Learn from Everyone

"Mature leaders listen, learn, and then they lead." –John Maxwell

Big Question: How can I be more teachable?

Homework:
☐ **Read** 1 John 5:11-12   2 Corinthians 5:17
John 1:12

4. Overcome Adversity

"It ain't about how hard you hit, it's about how hard you can get hit and keep moving forward." —Rocky Balboa

Big Question: What is the biggest trial from my past and toughest challenge facing me today?

Homework:

☐ **Write down every hard experience from your past.** If you have not addressed one, been healed from a past hurt, or are still struggling, consider talking with a counselor, pastor, coach, or close friend to make the next step in moving toward complete restoration.

☐ **Write down on an index card: "_____s (Your last name) never give up."** In your heart, embrace the adversities and challenges you have faced and are currently battling. Begin saying this to yourself and your family. We never give up.

5. Consistently Disconnect to Question, Think, and Write

"I want you to go on a quest to find yourself and the answers to life's questions." —Chad Simpson

Big Question: When will I withdraw to meet with the Father?

Homework:

☐ **Go to a quiet place** to listen, read, think, and write for 20-30 minutes.

☐ **Go one day without social media.**

6. Live for a Y Bigger than u

"Let your Y transcend u. Most purposes center on self, but there is something greater to live for." -Chad Simpson

Big Question: What is my purpose?

Homework:

☐ **Write down a purpose statement** for your life.

☐ **Write down three characteristics** to describe the type person that you want to become in 10 years.

7. Get Your BIG ROCKS in First

"Small things creep in and distract us from the important things. Each day, I want to get my Big Rocks in first. If there is extra time, then I am free to chase extras after the Big Rocks are accomplished." —Chad Simpson

Big Question: What are my top priorities?

Homework:

☐ **Write down your top three priorities** and read them in the morning. At night, look at them again, reflect, and journal about how well you pursued those priorities and what minor things distracted you from your Big Rocks.

8. Grow Your Grit Muscle

"Grit is like a muscle. The more you work it out, the stronger it becomes." –Chad Simpson

Big Question: What should I try that is out of my comfort zone?

Homework:

☐ **Do something you normally wouldn't do.** Perform a task, attend an event, or start a conversation that will be difficult. Get out of your comfort zone. Don't be afraid because this is where grit will grow. By facing smaller challenges with courage, you will have the confidence to face whatever life will throw at you.

9. Seek a Mentor

"Mentoring is a brain to pick, an ear to listen, and a push in the right direction." —John C. Crosby

Big Question: Who is investing in me?

Homework:

☐ **Find a mentor.** We all need someone who is a step ahead and willing to take their time to pour into us. Who is that for you? Take the first step and ask them, "Would you be willing to meet with me to talk about potentially being my mentor?" When you meet with them, be prepared with a list of 5-7 thoughtful and applicable questions. Then remember to: Listen and Learn from Everyone.

10. Choose Right Places

"Too many people say they want to surround themselves with quality, caring friends, but every week, they go to the wrong places."
—Chad Simpson

Big Question: Where do I need to go to be built up and encouraged to live out my identity, purpose, and priorities?

Homework:

☐ **Go to a "right place."** Just one time, take the first step and go to that new or familiar environment. You know the place. It is where you know God wants you to go. Here, you will find positive peer pressure to do what is right.

11. Express Gratitude to Loved Ones

"A turtle on a fence post did not get there by himself." – Unknown

Big Question: Who has impacted me to be where I am today?

Homework:

☐ **Write three "Thank you" notes or messages** to people you are thankful for. In it, be specific. Tell them what they do and how it makes your feel. And if you do not tell your loved ones, "I love you," begin today to tell them you love them.

12. Give your All—and Then Some

"There is no secret sauce to success. You just have to grind, outwork the competition, and find that little extra that no one else is willing to do." –Chad Simpson

Big Question: Where can I give more effort?

Homework:

☐ **Do more than what is asked.** Whatever has been asked of you, go find something more to do. Not so that anyone will notice, but only for you to know in your heart that you gave your all—and then some.

13. Fuel your High-Performance Sports Car

"We treat our nice cars with luxury treatment while feeding our bodies junk. And it's not only food. Think about the music, social media, movies, or shows you consume. Think about your sleep. All of these feed your body and mind, playing a major role in how strong you are." –Chad Simpson

Big Question: How can I better feed my body, my mind, and my soul?

Homework:

☐ **Unfollow everyone on social media who does not encourage, uplift, or add value to your life.**

14. Serve YOUR Team

"Your skills and talents are not about you. Look around you. They are your purpose. They are why you are here. It's not about you." –Chad Simpson

Big Question: What team or person can I serve today?

Homework:

☐ **Do one act of service today.**

15. Multiply

Success should be measured not by how many disciples are made, but by how many disciples are making other disciples." –Bill Hull

Big Question: Who do I need to consistently invest in?

Homework:

☐ **Find one person to disciple.** No matter where you have been or currently are, you can find someone to disciple. Walk with them through life. Meet with them to train and teach them. You don't have to have all the answers. You just need to be available for God to use you. The Lord will speak through you if you ask him. Do this until they are ready to go out and do the same with someone else. Through this multiplication process, we can change the world!

Notes

Introduction
1. National Center for Educational Statistics. "Back to school statistics." Accessed December 3, 2019. https://nces.ed.gov/fastfacts/display.asp?id=372

Chapter 8
1. Roosevelt, T. (n/d). Goodreads.com. Accessed on November 10, 2019. https://www.goodreads.com/quotes/34690-people-don-t-care-how-much-you-know-until-they-know.
2. Chartoff, R., Winkler, I., & Stallone, S. (2006). *Rocky Balboa*. United States: Columbia Pictures, Metro-Goldwyn-Mayer, and Revolution Studios.

Chapter 9
1. 1 Corinthians 15:33.
2. Maxwell, J. C. (2007). *The 21 Irrefutable Laws of Leadership: Follow Them and People will Follow You.* Nashville: Erikson Nelson, 2007.

Chapter 10
1. West, Erikson G., 1945-. (1979). *Plato's "Apology of Socrates"*: an interpretation, with a new translation. Ithaca, N.Y. :Cornell University Press.

Chapter 14
1. Craig Groeschel (@craiggroeschel). "Why we do what we do is important. People will work for a "what," but they'll give their lives for a "why."" Sep 1, 2017, 9:00 AM. Twitter. https://twitter.com/craiggroeschel/status/903603381624811520.

Chapter 16
1. Walmart Inc. "Our History." Accessed on November 11, 2019. https://corporate.walmart.com/our-story/our-history
2. Mission Statement Academy. "McDonald's Mission and Vision Statement Analysis." Accessed on July 15, 2019. https://mission-statement.com/mcdonalds/
3. Starbucks Coffee Company. "Our Mission." Accessed on November 10, 2019. https://www.starbucks.com/about-us/company-information/mission-statement
4. Google. "Our Approach to Search." Accessed on November 10, 2019. https://www.google.com/search/howsearchworks/mission/
5. Mary Kay. "Our Commitment." Accessed on November 10, 2019. https://www.marykay.com/en-us/about-mary-kay/our-commitment
6. Simon Sinek. (n.d.). AZQuotes.com. Accessed on November 11, 2019. https://www.azquotes.com/quote/708444

Chapter 17
1. James 1:1

Chapter 20
1. Angela Duckworth (n/d). Ted.com. Accessed November 11, 2019. https://www.ted.com/talks/angela_lee_duckworth_grit_the_power_of_passion_and_perseverance/transcript

Chapter 22
1. John Crosby. (n.d). BrainyQuote.com Accessed on May 14, 2020. https://www.brainyquote.com/quotes/john_c_crosby_137546

Chapter 25
1. Westering, F. *Make Big Time Where You Are.* Big Five Productions; updated 2nd edition, 2001.
2. Life Church (lifechurch). "If it's not God's time, you can't force it. When it is God's time, you can't stop it." - Craig Groeschel #hopeinthedark #lifechurch #wednesdaywisdom. 1 PM November 26, 2019. Twitter. https://twitter.com/lifechurch/status/1199387418555756545.

Chapter 28
1. Zhang, M. "How To Become So Good They Can't Ignore You." Last modified July 14, 2014. https://www.businessinsider.com/become-so-good-they-cant-ignore-you-2014-7.

Chapter 29
1. Quora.com. "Cars and Automobiles." Accessed on November 10, 2019. https://www.quora.com/How-much-is-the-maintenance-cost-of-the-Ferrari-488-GTB-and-Lamborghini-Aventador-in-India.
2. Cheryl D. Fryar, M.S.P.H., Jeffery P. Hughes, M.P.H., Kirsten A. Herrick, Ph.D., MSc., and Namanjeet Ahluwalia, Ph.D. "Fast Food Consumption Among Adults in the United States, 2013–2016." (October 2018) https://www.cdc.gov/nchs/products/databriefs/db322.htm.
3. www.dhhs.nh.gov. "How Much Sugar Do You Eat? You May Be Surprised!" Accessed on November 10, 2019. https://www.dhhs.nh.gov/dphs/nhp/documents/sugar.pdf.
4. Center for Disease Control and Prevention. "Only 1 in 10 Adults Get Enough Fruits or Vegetables" Accessed on November 16, 2019. https://www.cdc.gov/media/releases/2017/p1116-fruit-vegetable-consumption.html

Chapter 30
1. John Maxwell (n.d) Lampo Licensing. "Dave Rant: How to Finally Take Control of Your Money." Accessed on Novmeber 11, 2019.

https://www.daveramsey.com/blog/how-to-take-control-of-your-money.
2. Alcorn, Randy. *The Treasure Principle, Revised and Updated: Unlocking the Secret of Joyful Giving.* Portland, OR.: Multnomah Press, 2017.
3. Medicalnewstoday.com. "What are the benefits of eating healthy?" Accessed on November 10, 2019. https://www.medicalnewstoday.com/articles/322268.php4.
4. Healthline.com. "Experts Agree: Sugar Might Be as Addictive as Cocaine." Accessed November 10, 2019. https://www.healthline.com/health/food-nutrition/experts-is-sugar-addictive-drug

Chapter 31
1. John Wooden (n.d). GoodReads. "Quotable Quote." Accessed on November 10, 2019. https://www.goodreads.com/quotes/759536-talent-will-get-you-to-the-top-but-it-takes

Your Next Move
1. Maxwell, J. C. (2007). *The 21 Irrefutable Laws of Leadership: Follow Them and People will Follow You.* Nashville: Erikson Nelson, 2007.
2. Chartoff, R., Winkler, I., & Stallone, S. (2006). *Rocky Balboa.* United States: Columbia Pictures, Metro-Goldwyn-Mayer, and Revolution Studios.
3. Bill Hull. (n.d.). Mobilizing Disciples. Accessed on May 14, 2020. https://www.mobilizingdisciples.com/discipleship-quotes.html

Scriptures taken from the Holy Bible, New International Version®, NIV®. Copyright © 1973, 1978, 1984, 2011 by Biblica, Inc.™ Used by permission of Zondervan. All rights reserved worldwide. www.zondervan.com The "NIV" and "New International Version" are trademarks registered in the United States Patent and Trademark Office by Biblica, Inc.™

The Freshman

Acknowledgements

One of the best parts of writing this book was seeing how many people helped out on the journey. This project was a compilation of everyone who has influenced me and everyone who helped take it from an idea to a completed book. The initial idea was planted by my Lord and Savior, Jesus Christ, and my faith was stretched as I sought Him for help, ideas, and words along the way.

I could not have finished this project without the support from my wife, Emily. You listened to me for countless hours talk about this story, added so much to it through edits and revisions, and prayed for the hearts of the readers.

Thank you Mom, for being a huge support throughout my entire life. You were one of the first to read an early manuscript and believed that I could become an author.

Thank you Dad, for coaching me to be a better man, husband, dad, and coach. You have been in a courageous fight the past two years and through it all, have never complained but always cared, listened, and given advice.

I have so many family members, friends, teammates, leaders, pastors, coaches, and coworkers that have taught me lessons on my journey, but I want to thank three mentors that have intentionally invested in me on a weekly or monthly basis. Kurt Sovine pastored me in high school at a very pivotal time in my life to go the Father and to get involved in His mission. After I graduated college, Tim Johnson taught me so many lessons on leadership and sports ministry, but his enthusiasm and passion for the Gospel—God, Man, Christ, Response—was most impactful. Most recently, Phil Shomo taught me how to truly listen, love, and mentor. Your mentoring dug into my heart, emotions, and masculinity. And all three of you continue to pour into me today.

Finally, to the massive team who helped give feedback and edit this story. God connected me with so many people who took this from a messy rough draft to a published book. Cindy Katz, Daniel Peaslee, Aunt Rox, Gian Lemmi, Andy Millis, and Dr. Dycus. I cannot say thank you enough.

And to you my reader, thank you! The biggest gift you could give is to implement these lessons and share it with others.

About the Author

Chad absolutely loves being married to his bride of ten years, Emily, and being a father to their three children: Josiah (6), Abigail (4), and Stephen (1).

Chad has served as a coach for over 15 years. He was a record-breaking D1 athlete at Liberty University and is an award-winning collegiate coach. He speaks to colleges, high schools, and nonprofits, and is the current Assistant Athletic Director and Head Men's and Women's Tennis Coach at Point University in Georgia.

Connect with Chad:

Twitter: @CoachChadS
Instagram: @CoachChadSimpson
Email: coachchadsimpson1@gmail.com

Made in the USA
Columbia, SC
05 May 2025